THE GET ALONG GUIDE
DEEPER INTO GOD'S WORD. DEEPER INTO RELATIONSHIP.

DANIELLE MACAULAY

Copyright © 2020 Danielle Macaulay
All rights reserved.
ISBN: 9798673076736

THANK YOU

Thank you, Bill Farrel, for not only helping me sound waaaay more intelligent than I am, but for gifting me with so much history, truth and insight behind the words in the scriptures we used for this study. I am well aware how privileged I am that you've welcomed me in as your student. You have helped me hone my craft, challenged me to dig deeper and "try again" and you've built my confidence as a writer tremendously. I thank you for all you've given me, and I promise to pass it on to the next "up and comer". You and Pam are the "real deal" in the book world and in all of life. #besteditorever

Thank you, Mom for giving of yourself sacrificially yet again. All those years working in a library surrounded by books, and your wonderfully nit-picky proofreading skills came in handy for this project! I love you!

Thank you, Dan….well, for everything. You make me better in every way, and you've definitely made this project look better than I certainly could have…and most likely better than anyone else I would have hired for the job. We will discuss payment. ;) I love you, I love you, I love you.

CONTENTS

About This Study 7
Opening 9

Section 1 - "Relationship Spoilers"

Session 1 - Prejudjement and Pride 13
Session 2 - Jealousy/Envy and Comparison 31
Session 3 - Competition and Insecuirty 47
Session 4 - Misunderstandings and Unforgiveness 61

Section 2 - "God's Recipe for Relashionship Success"

Session 5 - A Pinch of Patience and a Cup of Confession 79
Session 6 - An Ounce of Openness and a Teaspoon of Truth 95
    A Smidgeon of Service and a Litre of Love
Session 7 - A Dash of Discretion, Blend in Blessing 109
Session 8 - A Gram of Gratitude and a Quart of Confidence 123

Section 3 - "Consequences" (of not getting along) and "What Happens When We All Get Along."

Session 9 - The Consequences of disunity 137
Session 10 - Unity 151
    Get your girls together, everyone bring one of their favorite "appetizer" recipes, and enjoy them and each other! Share about how God has transformed you and your relationships!

THE GET ALONG TRIO

WHY CAN'T WE ALL JUST GET ALONG?!
A RECIPE FOR SUCCESS IN YOUR RELATIONSHIPS
DANIELLE MACAULAY

The book that started it all. Begin your journey here or catch up now!
GETALONGGIRL.COM

THE GET ALONG GUIDE
DEEPER INTO GOD'S WORD. DEEPER INTO RELATIONSHIP.
DANIELLE MACAULAY

Go even deeper into The Word, make it personal, and grow!

Grab The Get Along Video Group Guide!
Short videos from Danielle designed to turn the guide you're holding into the perfect small-group study! Get it at:
GETALONGGUIDE.COM

ABOUT THIS STUDY

I've received some really great advice in my life. Tips like, "Always follow through on commitments" or "Don't pluck your grey hairs out or two will grow back in its place." And, of course "Don't eat after 8pm - not a Rice, or a Krispie." Those may or may not all be true, but none of that advice will change my life forever.

The Bible, however, is jam packed with wisdom and practical advice from the One who makes this entire operation happen. God created this world, and He formed you and me in our mother's belly. So, without a doubt, He's got the inside scoop on the best way to live. My desire has always been to live righteously, but my own sinful tendencies and the brokenness of this world can bring me down. Applying God's truth to my life has always been the answer to lift me back up to where I need to be.

The Get Along Guide contains all the truth of God's word that has helped me heal, overcome and be victorious in my relationships. No, I am not anywhere close to perfection - and neither are my relationships, but God's involvement in my life has certainly kept me from heartache, frustration and heaps of trouble. So, let my advice be to you, "The Bible will offer you life to the fullest...and prevent you from growing unnecessary grey hairs." I think we can all agree that sounds pretty desirable.

As you travel through these pages, my prayer is that you and your relationships will be changed forever. Here are a few tips to help you get the max benefits from The Get Along Guide...

1. First of all, grab some girlfriends to journey through this book together with you. Accountability is a good thing, and you'll have much more fun. My video group guide will help you along the way!

2. Next, I urge you to snag yourself a copy of *Why Can't We All Just*

Get Along!? from Amazon or my website: **frommilktomeat.com**. The study you're holding in your hands is the Bible Study Companion to that book. I promise that your experience will be elevated when you have all the information from both books combined.

3. Be diligent and committed to the process. There are 10 sessions included in this study which are all easily completed within a week. Each session includes these components:

- Get Into It - An introduction to the topic of the session.
- Get Insight - My personal insights on the topic.
- Get Inspiration - Instructions from God's Word on each topic.
- Get Intentional - Your turn to reflect and respond.

I encourage you to take your time and not just breeze through the pages. Instead, ask God to reveal in you what needs to be changed and dive in with an open heart. I wholeheartedly believe that the contents of this study has the ability to radically change your thoughts, attitudes, actions and your entire life. Here we go!

GET ALONG GUIDE

Opening

I watched with dread and suspense, a video of a lion about to attack two gazelles to their death. It was all out in open space. There was no hiding, sudden attack or pouncing involved. The Lion had a clear view and darted towards them from football fields away.

"Football fields away!?" You ask! "Wasn't there any time for the gazelles to run for cover?" We're talking about animals that could keep up with a Volvo on the freeway, and yet the Lion devoured them before they knew it. This is why:

The gazelles were locking horns. They were heads down, engaging in war with one another, making each other the enemy. Now, gazelles don't fight to devour each other, but to dominate over and dispute each other.

The two gazelles were much too busy locking horns, that they were completely distracted and blinded to their *real* enemy - the one coming from afar to devour them both.

And devour them he did. That Lion took them both down in an instant. Faster than I could believe, really. I couldn't stop watching though.

Neither could a few onlookers. I noticed in the foreground of the video, two other gazelles sitting quietly, observing the whole thing. They were at a safe distance for now, not the target of the predator, and so they took it all in. They watched the fight, and then they watched the attack.

Girls, we are under attack. We are being hunted down and there is someone who is laser focused on devouring us.

Some of us are busy though. Many of us are involved in dominating over and disputing one another. Others are distracted with unforgiveness and waging war with "her" in their heads. Too many of us are competing against each other, when we should be rallying together to fight the real enemy.

> Too many of us are competing against each other, when we should be rallying together to fight the real enemy.

The devil does wear Prada, girls. He is keen to disguise himself and make us believe that the one we should be at odds with is "her" - but really, it's him.

This "Get Along Guide" Bible Study companion to my book, *Why Can't We All Just Get Along* is designed to be your weapon against the real enemy. God's word is our most powerful tool to fight Satan, and so we must use it accordingly.

John 10:10 warns us that Satan comes to steal, kill and destroy. He's out for you, and he's out for the church. He wants us distracted and divided. He knows that when united, we are an indestructible and unstoppable force for the Kingdom of God.

John 13:35 says that the World will know that we are Jesus' disciples...and I would add that, as a result, they will know Him by our love for one another.

So, there is a lot riding on the way we view and treat one another. When we can truly be unified and get along the way God has commanded us to, we not only save ourselves, but we save a dying world.

The churches of the new testament were encouraged and exhorted time and time again to "get along". Their leaders knew that there was a lot riding on how they viewed and treated each other as well.

Write down the instructions to the churches about being unified in these verses:

1 Corinthians 1:10 _____
_____

2 Corinthians 13:11 _____
_____

Philippians 2:2 _____
_____

Colossians 3:14 _____
_____
_____

1 Peter 3:8 _____
_____
_____

And now, I am encouraging and challenging you to equip yourself to love and be unified with the women around you - not as best as *you* can, but alongside The One who's power can defeat any prowling lion.

SESSION 1

Spoiler # 1 - Prejudgement

Get Into It

I was surprised to find out that we judge others in the first six seconds of our interaction with them (Catrina Welch, Confident Beauty). Do you believe this? Now that I think about it, I sure do, and it gives new force to the old saying, "Don't judge a book by it's cover". Here's an example of the absurdity we surmise....

She's overweight = She must be lazy
She's on a stage - She must be full of herself
She's with Her - She must be a snob
She's a blond bombshell = She must have great self confidence
She's toting that high end purse = She must be materialistic
She's always smiling on Instagram = She's living a charmed life
(From *"Why Can't We All Just Get Along?!"* p. 12)

In the space below, describe a time you reached an inaccurate conclusion about another woman based upon your first impression of her.

_____
_____
_____
_____
_____

Ladies, there is a better way to view our sisters in Christ, and the ones who could be. Let's dig into the best way to learn how to turn our judgements and discriminations into tolerance, acceptance and love.

Get Inspiration

Find **James 2:1-7**. Who does James suggest we become like if we show partiality to others based on outward things?

_____

What type of thoughts does James say we have when we judge others?

_____

Think about a time when you have shown partiality to (or discrimination/judgement against) someone based on their outward appearance, circumstances in life, or simply from the limited information you know of them.

We usually believe our summations and opinions are the superior ones. I'll be the first to admit that I can be a real "know it all" too. Over time though, I've discovered that I can be vastly wrong about people I thought I had pegged pretty accurately. And, I'm even more wrong when I treat them according to my judgements.

Now, flip back a bit to **Matthew 7:1-5**. Record verses 1 and 2 here:

_____

_____

_____

In Jesus' most famous sermon, He makes it very clear that whether we judge based on accurate summations or not, we put ourselves in harm's way of being judged ourselves.

What does **Romans 2:1-3** say about the same thing? _____

_____
_____
_____

If we try to do God's job (judging) for Him, we risk being "called out" ourselves **(Luke 6:37)**. Always err on the side of grace - for her sake, and for your own. Jesus is continually showing me that I don't have it all figured out and I need to keep my "grace lenses" on when looking at even my dearest friends. My vision is blurred by my sin.

Get Insight

One of my pastors told us a funny story with a great truth attached to it. He was sifting through some junk in the trunk of his car in his Bible College parking lot. While doing so, he was biting down on a white Bic pen, half of it sticking out of his mouth. Another student saw him from afar, and immediately reported him for smoking on campus. After explaining himself to the Dean that the "cigarette" was just a ball point pen, he realized an important life lesson that he'd carry with

> Believe none of what you hear and only half of what you see.

him through life: *believe none of what you hear and only half of what you see. Even our own eyes can deceive us!*

Just like that woman was way off base about our pastor smoking on the Bible College campus, we can be way off base about other women. Our eyes, ears, mind, past experiences and our heart can all deceive us. So, when you look at the women around you, make sure to remember your grace lenses and keep an open heart and mind!

Get Intentional

Growing up, I never liked the meaning of my name. It sounded negative and scary. The meaning of the name "Danielle" is "God is my judge". A funny thing happened - I grew up and married a boy named Dan. His real name, "Daniel" has the same meaning as mine. When I shared with him that I'd always thought negatively that God is my judge, he said that he had always felt the opposite way. He was glad that God is his judge, because He is a merciful one.

God extends us grace and views us through loving eyes. He sees the best in us. He judges us fairly and lovingly. Phew! Once I thought about things that way, I was so relieved.

Wouldn't it be great if we all judged others the same way - with grace, eyes of love and an attitude of exemption. Wouldn't we all benefit from seeing and believing the best in others?

In order to do that, here are some questions that can help you ponder how you have viewed other women:

How would you have felt if you were the one being accused of "smoking a white pen"? _____

_____

_____

Has there been a time that I "sized her up" before I got to know her?

What is that relationship like now? _____
_____
_____

When have I felt wrongly judged? How did it make me feel? What is my relationship with that person like today? _____
_____
_____
_____

Who, or what situation could I be misled about? _____
_____
_____

Who can I give a second chance to? _____
_____
_____

How do I put on my "Grace Lenses" in order to view others in a non-judgemental way? _____
_____
_____
_____

How do I clean my "Grace Lenses" when they get dirty? _____

The Get Along Guide

_____
_____
_____

What is my prescription for my "Grace Lenses"? _____
_____
_____

We are all more alike than different. We all carry hidden hurts and long to be accepted. The first step to loving and accepting another woman is to be open to learning who they truly are without letting judgement creep in.

I believe that the Holy Spirit will lead us to the right people we should have close relationship with and will steer us clear of people who are not safe to bring into our inner circle. But, for the most part, when we prematurely judge based on outer appearances or our own hangups, we miss out on the blessing of a great relationship.

> *"Do not judge, or you too will be judged."*
> **Matthew 7:1**

Spoiler # 2 - Pride

Get Into It

While I was surprised to find out that we judge people within the first 6 seconds of knowing them, I am well aware that 100% of us battle pride. Yet, in Carey Neiwhof's book *Didn't See It Coming*, we learn that pride is expressed in different ways, and is a sneaky one to catch.

> *"Pride disguises itself in many ways. It's so pervasive that it has to be subtle. If we only knew one form we'd stop it dead in its tracks. So it spawns. Pride morphs and it creeps in using methods that often go unnoticed."*[1]

The hardest people to detect pride in is ourselves. Of course, a narcissist never believes they are proud because they are always right! The rest of us, however, will be greatly helped by the subtle cues that point to pride. Pride is easy to spot when it is characterized by loud, boastful, in your face annoyances. It is much harder to recognize when it puts on disguises.

> The first step to loving and accepting another woman is to be open to learning who they truly are without letting judgement creep in.

When boiled down, pride is simply selfishness. In it's worst form, it is an obsession with self. It thinks of itself first and best, and in the meantime, it leaves our Lord out of the picture. Yes, pride promotes and protects itself. But, it also:

- Masquerades as mere superficiality, while seeking attention and neglecting others
- Conceals itself as a critical spirit, and in our irritation with others.
- Disguises itself in defensiveness and fault finding, causing us to filter out the evils in ourselves and the good in others.
- Wraps itself up in worry and fear.

Pride's most drastic deception is insecurity. Those obnoxious "know it alls" you know are usually deeply entangled in and gripped by uncertainty about themselves or about God - and are doing everything they can to conceal that, most of the time subconsciously.

Yes, the tall tree of pride has roots of insecurity. While they seem to blow and grow in polar opposite directions, they are equally destructive. Pride stands tall, overshadowing others, while insecurity stays buried away from others.

> The tall tree of pride has roots of insecurity.

We must understand that they are two sides of the same coin - obsession with self. This mindset holds zero value in our lives. Instead, it costs us a great deal in our relationships. Both pride and insecurity are imbalanced, unhealthy views of ourselves and God.

So, let's allow the Word of God to bring us back into balance, with a healthy view of who we are (and aren't), and who God is.

We will uproot insecurity later in this study, but for now let's discuss how much our pride could cost us…

Get Insight

Dive into these verses to uncover what God's word says will happen when you decide you don't need Him, and that you've got it covered. Write them down in the space provided below.

Galatians 6:3 _____

_____

_____

Proverbs 11:2 _____
_____
_____

Proverbs 26:12 _____
_____
_____

James 4:6 _____
_____
_____

Psalm 138:6 _____
_____
_____

Philippians 2:3 _____
_____
_____

1 Corinthians 13:4 _____
_____
_____

Things aren't looking up for prideful folk, are they? And yet, here I am, guilty of pride in my heart on a regular basis. I admit there's times I am prideful of my mothering choices, my daily habits, my relationship with my spouse, my body and so much more.

When I think I'm better than other women, it's not only harmful for me, but for my relationships. I immediately construct a wall between me and them. "I am better than you and I don't need you" is a risky decision to make.

> If we're not careful... our strength will actually work against us.

Pride isolates us from others. It is in that isolation where the enemy can best convince you of his lies. So, God is clear that He won't allow us to remain in a prideful place for long. It is too unsafe - the edge, right before a fall.

Oswald Chambers says *"an unguarded strength is a double weakness"*. [2] This says to me, that if we're not careful to guard our hearts against being proud of our strengths, and give God the glory - that our strength will actually work against us.

The following are strong, wealthy and powerful people the Lord dealt with as they became "too big for their britches"...

Get Inspiration

Read the entirety of Obadiah. I promise you, it's not more than a page or two in your bible - a tiny book sandwiched between Amos and Jonah. If you do not have time, bypass to verses 12 and 13.

What were the sins of Edom? In my version, I see the words "gloated and spoken arrogantly (boasted)". The folks of Edom were a proud bunch. They were deceived by their own pride, says verse three. They thought they were untouchable up in their "rock fortress high in the mountains". They were even daring enough to rejoice when others experienced destruction.

How do you think the other cities viewed the people of Edom? Would their hearts be tender and favorable towards them? Would they have their respect, or their contempt? This leads me to wonder how others perceive me when pride seeps out of my pores. What about you? I'm assuming it would not be well received.

It seems Edom thought they would be exempt from harm; that they were untouchable. Yet, how did God Almighty respond to their pride? Write out God's response in your own words in the following verses:

v2. _____

_____

v4. _____

_____

v8. _____

_____

God clearly wasn't messing around. He said that when we allow pride in our hearts, we take on some of the same characteristics as the fallen angel... the one who thought he too was above God (**Ezekiel 28**). Indeed, pride came before his fall.

Sift through the first 8 verses of **Ezekiel 28**. The description of the Prince of Tyre here sounds awfully and dreadfully familiar to that of Lucifer. And, even worse I see snippets of myself in there too. Verses 7 and 8 seem to be a confirmation of what we read in **Proverbs 11:2**.

Rewrite the words of **Proverbs 11:2**: _____
_____
_____

Sum up **Ezekiel 28:1-8** in your own words here: _____
_____
_____

Let's continue on to another example of pride preceding a fall - a big fall. Read **2 Chronicles 26:16-23**. If you are in a group, have someone read it aloud.

> We are responsible to reign in our pride, so God doesn't have to do it for us.

King Uzziah was a prosperous man, who became famous for his strength and knowledge. He had special knowledge to conceive and construct weapons, which made him known far and wide. At the age of 16 years old he was made king and he began to rule, replacing his father.

He makes me immediately think of child celebrities, and how young fame messes with them. It has been said that child stars often remain at the maturity level of the years they rose to stardom for the rest of their life! Any human has a hard time staying grounded with this type of adoration, let alone someone put in that position from such a young age. Still, we are responsible to reign in our pride, so God doesn't have to do it for us.

Eventually, Uzziah took his eyes off the Lord and kept them on himself. He lost consciousness that God was responsible for his success. He viewed himself as superior to God, even believing he could alter the way in which worship was to be conducted.

Write down the result of King Uzziah's prideful, disobedient actions. (v 21) _____

_____

_____

Now turn to the book of Daniel. Read chapter 4:28-33.

King Neb had "grown strong and great" (v 22) so much so, that his greatness "reaches up to the heavens" and "rules to the end of the earth". It would be a cinch to believe you deserve adoration with this kind of power and influence. So, if we don't keep ourselves in check, we will soon forget about God and put ourselves in jeopardy like King Neb. Write down his words in verse 30:

_____

_____

_____

_____

I see "I" and "my" in there, but... zero "God" recognition.

What was the result of King Neb's pride? (v 31-33)

_____

_____

_____

The Kings of the Old Testament are certainly drastic examples of people being put in their proper place. But, most of us would agree that we never want to be humbled, no matter the severity.

From the beginning of time, we see examples of pride preceding a fall. The heading of Genesis chapter 3 in my Bible is entitled "The Fall".

Sure enough, Eve is tempted by Satan to question, and then disobey God. How he lures her in is with the idea that she too, will be like God - all knowing. Read verses 4-6 and record verse 6 here:

_____

_____

_____

Perhaps we can relate with Eve. We all are tempted at times to be the lord of our own lives, and lord over others. Our pride lures us away into dangerous territory, that at the time seems desirable, but in the end leaves us regretful and looking and feeling foolish.

An acquaintance told me about a time her friend taught her the sign language for a popular worship song. Every time it was sung at church, she would sign along with the song, hoping to make it seem she was more fluent than she was. One day, her pastor asked her to come to the stage to teach her congregation the signs. This made her heart swell with pride that she would be centered out to do that. After the service though, a family with a deaf member in it approached her, frustrated that she was teaching it incorrectly. Of course, she couldn't understand all of what the deaf man was trying to communicate with her, but she got the gist. She said she went from feeling proud to totally defeated and embarrassed. She was certainly knocked down a few pegs.

A friend of mine was also knocked down a few pegs on picture day. This is how her story unfolded:

"When I was in highschool, I wanted to prepare for picture day by obliterating my pimple by drinking 8 glasses of water within minutes the night before. Not sure where I heard that one! I ended up throwing up and my mom came running in and flushed the toilet right away as she tried to comfort/pray for me. When I looked up and

smiled at her we realized my retainer (which included a false tooth) had been flushed down the toilet. Needless to say, the pimple wasn't even a thought the following day as I did my best to keep my mouth closed all day! The photo that year was probably the only school photo I ever had with a closed smile!"

Yikes! Pride really does trip us up.

It is much better that we remain low, allowing Jesus to be the focal point of our lives. In *Why Can't We All Just Get Along?!* I share a story of how my brother in law explained to us that when a donkey becomes prideful, it will puff itself up and kick itself up on its hind legs in order to appear bigger than he is. He suggested that if the donkey who carried Jesus at His triumphal entry became proud in that moment, he would have let Jesus fall right off his back.

> It is much better that we remain low, allowing Jesus to be the focal point of our lives.

A small fraction of us are wealthy, powerful and famous. Most of us are just everyday donkeys. But, a large fraction of us have "let Jesus fall off our backs" on one occasion or another. Whether it be our food, fashion or our faith choices, let's be careful to remember who gives us every good thing - even our ability to choose.

It is imperative that we keep our pride in check by remembering and acknowledging where our gifts and blessings originate. Let's do that now.

Get Intentional

So, let's check our hearts...

Ask the Lord to search and examine your heart and test if there is any wicked way (**Psalm 139: 23, 24**). Give yourself a few moments to be able to distinguish what the Lord may be speaking to you. Perhaps it's clear, but maybe you need to dig deep.

First, tell me what you consider to be your greatest strengths, abilities and blessings. What talents / resources /characteristics do you have? What are you good at? What special qualities do people recognize in you? List some here: _____

_____

_____

Who gave you the wisdom, ability, finances, resources to have or achieve these things or qualities? _____

_____

_____

Take these scriptures in:

> *"Every good and perfect gift is from above,*
> *coming down from the father of heavenly lights."*
> **James 1:17**

> *"Naked I came from my mother's womb;*
> *and naked I will depart. The Lord gave and He has*
> *taken away; may the name of The Lord be praised."*
> **Job 1:21**

Any good thing we possess in this life is directly from the hand of God, and can be snatched away in a moment's notice. He is our source.

What areas of your life have you maybe let some pride creep in? When have you "let Jesus fall off your back? Write them down:

___

Are these some of the same things that you listed on the last page that can be counted as your strengths, gifts and abilities?

___

God's feelings on pride aren't just reserved for the rich, famous and powerful. He is speaking to you and me today. You've identified some areas that you think God may be wanting you to surrender in humility to him. How can you act upon that? What practical ways can you make Him famous through what He's given you?

Share some personal thoughts here about how you can alter the specifics of your life (time, talents, behaviors, speech, mind...) to make it all about Him and less about you.

___

Our pride not only stains our hearts and muddies our relationships, it forces Jesus into the dirt. Like I mentioned earlier, when we act like proud donkeys and forget what we're supposed to be about, Jesus slides off our backs, unseen. Ladies, let's never assume that we are the main event, lest we ever let Jesus land in the dirt behind us.

> *"A proud (wo)man is always looking down on things and people. As long as you're looking down, you can't see something above you."* [3]
> C.S. Lewis

Session 2

Spoiler # 3 - Jealousy / Envy

Get Into It

The Bible describes jealousy and envy as what we know today about cancer. It can start small, but left to linger, it takes over and debilitates us. In time, if unaddressed, it will be the end of us. **Proverbs 27:4** says that wrath is cruel, anger is overwhelming, but who can stand before jealousy?" And, **Proverbs 14:3** tells us that jealousy "rots the bones". Jealousy is a state of misery. It has certainly soured my mood on many occasions.

From experience, I know that jealousy also makes you:

- feel insecure
- think irrationally
- look pathetic
- act selfishly
- pout
- blame God

At times jealousy has even stolen my sleep and made me feel sick to my stomach. Ultimately, we resemble the Wicked Witch of the West, green with envy and plagued with hate, and we make the ones we're jealous of into our enemies.

What else does **James 3:16** say tags along with jealousy (selfish ambition) and envy?

_____
_____
_____
_____

Get Insight

It's easy to think we're living holy lives if we don't curse like a sailor, sleep around or play with a Ouija board. But, buried deep down in our hearts there may be evil and disorder of every kind.

Galatians 5:19 couples jealousy along with the sins of lustful pleasures, sorcery and drunkenness. Warnings against envy (coveting) are also included in The 10 Commandments (**Exodus 20:17**).

> It is sin that separates us from God, no matter which way its sliced.

It is sin that separates us from God, no matter which way it is sliced. And, Satan keeps a hold on us when we choose to dwell in our sinful nature. **Ephesians 4:27** warns us not to let the devil get a foothold (an advantage, or strong position over us) by steering clear of, rather than mingling in sin.

In *Why Can't We All Just Get Along?!*, I describe the differences between envy and jealousy, but the constant is that both are strong emotions that are difficult to rid ourselves of. We need the power of the Holy Spirit to help us, otherwise envy and jealousy easily latch onto our hearts and take hold. When they grip our hearts, they choke out our peace and cause wars among us. It's a tale as old as time. Listen to the clear frustration in James in the letter he writes to the Jewish Christians:

> *"What is causing the quarrels and fights among you? Don't they come from the evil desires at war within you? You want what you don't have, so you scheme and kill to get it. You are jealous of what others have, but you can't get it so you fight and wage war to take it away from them. Yet you don't have what you want because you don't ask God for it. And even when you ask, you don't get it because your motives are all wrong - you only want what gives you pleasure"* **James 4:1-3**

You and I both know that we are sometimes still "waging war" on each other today, even if just within our hearts. Remember that the "Cold Wars" among us are just as destructive as the ones plainly seen - and if not dealt with, will evolve into full on warfare. If you need some convincing, check out the story of Saul...

Get Inspiration

Pick up your Bible and flip the pages to 1 Samuel 15. Read verses 24-28. What happened to Saul as a result of his disobedience?

_____
_____

Write down the painful words of the last half of verse 28.

_____
_____

He was not only rejected, but it was made clear to him, "someone better than you" will fill the role.

This is painful. Can you imagine hearing those words from the one who had gone before you and anointed you as King?

Now, peruse over to chapter 16:14-23 and take a look. A young, talented and "easy on the eyes" dude enters Saul's life. Even Saul is initially captivated by him.

Skip ahead to chapter 18:1-16. Carefully read through these verses.

Saul went from adoring and needing David, to despising him, with a jealous heart.

List some of the reasons why you think Saul became jealous of David:

_____
_____
_____
_____

There are many reasons Saul might have hated David. His own children loved and devoted themselves to David, as he continued to outshine their father. Jealousy and envy are easy emotions to acquire, but hard ones to escape. It takes resolve and intentionality.

Get Intentional

Some of you are trapped in a similar mindset as Saul. You may also have countless reasons to justify your feelings and give you false permission to feel right about them. But, please take this in:

When we over-focus on someone else's blessing it takes our eyes off of our own blessing, and keeps us miserable.

Spend a few moments digesting the last sentence, and then write down 5 blessings God has gifted you with:

1. _____
2. _____
3. _____
4. _____
5. _____

> When we over-focus on someone else's blessing it takes our eyes off of our own blessing

An attitude of gratitude is effective in flushing jealousy and envy out of our systems. We will discuss this more in part 2, session 7.

Another remedy for ridding our resentfulness towards other women is to be intentional to pay her a compliment! I know - this isn't what you were expecting me to say. But, the truth is that cheering her on will cheer you up!

Track with me.

Here's why: *Right feelings follow right actions.* We can train our mind to think righteous thoughts by doing righteous deeds (and then, vice versa). Most of the time our actions flow out of our thought life, but sometimes when our thoughts are in the gutter, we must will ourselves in the other direction by doing what we'd rather not do. Eventually, our feelings will catch up. Rather than running from the women we struggle with, when we run to them and bless them, we steer our hearts in the right direction.

Who do you struggle with that you can bless today? Write that name down here, and then start by paying her a compliment on this page.

Her name: _____

A Compliment for her: _____
_____
_____

I encourage you to follow that up with telling her. Next, why don't you try this:

Turn your envy into inspiration

In the column below, on the left hand side, write the things that you envy in her. In the column on the right hand side, jot down how those things can inspire you to be a better version of you, rather than wishing you were more like her. Turning your envy into inspiration is turning your "Woe is me, I'm not like her" into "Wow! Look at her! I admire those qualities." Do you see the difference? This is very freeing.

Enviable	**Inspiration to grow**
_____	_____
_____	_____
_____	_____
_____	_____
_____	_____

If we allow ourselves a God-sized perspective shift, we will actually be able to learn and grow from the ones we envy, rather than harbor hate in our hearts over them. I pray that you're beginning to see that she is not the enemy near as much as our own negative thought patterns.

"Jealousy rots the bones" **Proverbs 14:3**

But...

"A cheerful heart is good medicine" **Proverbs 17:22**

Spoiler # 4 - COMPARISON

Get Into It

I asked women on Facebook what they compare about themselves to other women. You name it and we compare it - our careers, how we raise our children, our house cleaning/cooking capabilities, our clothes, our weight, our sex appeal and how our husbands treat us - even our spirituality. We compare everything from our families to our fingernails.

But, we can't fully put the blame on ourselves. We live in a competitive world. Everywhere we turn, we are encouraged to scrutinize each other.

American Idol paved the way for this generation to master the art of picking people apart and comparing the intricacies of their looks, talent and personality with the "competition". Popular celebrity gossip magazine "Us Weekly" regularly includes a "Who wore it best?" page, featuring two women side by side, wearing the same outfit. Viewers are encouraged to vote for who wore it best. The writers analyze features from beads to bags, butts to boobs and everything in-between. Is there really ever a winner in these games? Unfortunately, these games are centuries old and are not fading any time soon. (*Why Can't We All Get Along?!* p. 41)

Get Insight

We were just discussing that King Saul's downfall was jealousy. I have come to understand that what often ignites the fires of jealousy and envy is comparison. There was a song written about King Saul and David, the one he was jealous of. Read **1 Samuel 18:7**. Write down the lyrics of the Isrealite Women's song here:

_____
_____
_____
_____
_____

Ouch. Sometimes we compare ourselves, and other times people do the dirty work for us. I wonder if the Isrealite women owned copies of "Us Weekly".

It is difficult to resist measuring our defeats and deficiencies against others, especially when others are highlighting them - and vocalizing it. Devastatingly, this is how the world operates. We are inundated with a comparison mentality and encouraged us to stack ourselves against one another.

Satan uses this to his advantage. He wants us to perpetually feel like we don't measure up, or he wants pride to burst within our hearts. He encourages us to compare ourselves with the "competition" and get sucked into his lies. He wants us to come to conclusions like, "Well, if *she's* doing it, and doing it better, then I might as well not even bother." This way, we'll throw in the towel, or seek to throw hers in for her. He distracts us from completing our mission.

This is exactly what happened to Saul. He enjoyed success, but there may have been so much more for him. He became distracted from his mission and was ousted from his position by becoming consumed with someone else's blessings and abilities. Rather than defeating the enemy, Saul defeated himself - and spiraled downward. Chapter 19 gives full evidence of that.

> Rather than defeating the enemy, Saul defeated himself.

Get Inspiration

Let's redirect our attention to **Numbers 13**.

Many of us know the story of Moses leading the Israelites through the desert to the "Promised Land"... the place flowing with milk and honey. If you aren't familiar with it, I encourage you to take the extra time and gobble up the story throughout Numbers and Deuteronomy. I won't rehash the details, but let's just say that they were beggars who tried to be choosers.

Similarly to myself at times, they were ungrateful for the provisions that the Lord had given them. They quickly forgot all that God had done for them and continually expected more. And, if this wasn't enough, when we look closely, we'll see that they too, fell into the comparison trap.

Read **Numbers 13:25-33**.

What did the "scouters" find when they were peering into Canaan's land?

___

Verse 27 reports that this place was indeed a land "flowing with milk and honey". It was a bountiful land, filled with powerful men who lived in large and fortified towns. Sounds a tad bit better than the living conditions the Israelites had been enduring, don't you think?

When it was suggested to go "take the land", what was the response of 10 of 12 the men who had explored the land? (V 31 and 33)

___

"They are stronger than we are"

"Next to them *we felt like grasshoppers."*

This sounds an awful lot like the Israelites got caught in the comparison trap.

What was the conclusion that the men who had explored made? (**Numbers 14:4**)

_____
_____
_____
_____

Once they decided that the Cannanites were stronger then they were, which in turn made them feel like tiny, weak, insignificant insects, they decided to pack it in. "Let's just choose a new leader and go back to Egypt", they whined.

Even after all they had endured, their comparisons drove them to call it quits and head back into slavery. Somehow that seemed like a better option to them.

There were two men in the group who had a differing opinion than the rest. Read **Numbers 14:8** and write down Joshua and Caleb's thoughts, despite the giants:

_____
_____
_____
_____

Skip back to **Exodus 33:11**. One of the spies who believed they could succeed in their mission (in the face of giants) was Joshua. Where does **Exodus 33:11** say that Joshua spent time and didn't want to leave?

_____
_____
_____
_____

The best way for us to remember what God says about us is to spend time listening to Him.

> Our God confidence will keep us from feeling the need to tower over others or cower under them.

Joshua seemingly spent copious amounts of time in the tent where the presence of the Lord was. I imagine that is where he realized who God was and who he was. And, once he heard from Almighty God, some dudes who had a few inches on him weren't about to squash him like a bug.

It is good for us to continually remind ourselves of who God says we are, It's so much more than we give ourselves credit for. Then, it won't matter who we are compared to. Our God confidence will keep us from feeling the need to tower over others, or cower under them.

Get Intentional

Maybe you identify with those spies. Perhaps at times you feel tiny, like a grasshopper next to a "giant" of a gal. Have you let comparison creep in and keep you from *your* "Promised Land"?

Examine yourself: are you spending too much time and brainpower exploring, or "scouting out" the ladies you believe are living in their "bountiful" land? My guess is yes, because we all fall knee deep into the pit of the practice of comparison if we aren't careful to steer clear of the trenches we have plowed for ourselves.

You may cringe, but I want you to write down the names of women who you have spent too much time and attention "spying" on. Who have you been comparing your looks, marriage, children, talents, successes and failures with?

Write their names here: _____

_____

_____

_____

If you can muster up the bravery, I challenge you to share that name with a trusted confidant - someone who can encourage you in who God made you to be, and challenge you to focus on your own blessings, calling and Promised Land.

Record what you believe your "Promised Land" is. What has God promised and gifted you with?

_____

_____

_____

_____

Now, how has focusing on others taken your eyes off that prize?

_____

_____

_____

_____

Here's why it's important to focus on our own journey, and not be distracted and discouraged by others: The Israelites spent 40 days checking the Canaanites out. And yes, what they did discover was that they were strong. Yet, that strength did not make the promise of the Lord null and void in the lives of the Israelites.

God led them, a pillar of cloud by day and fire by night. He sent manna. He promised, and he provided. The Israelites were his chosen. But, when they spent too much time comparing, they lost sight of God's promises for their lives. Remember that just because God has gifted another woman does not mean He has not gifted you as well.

> Just because God has gifted another woman does not mean He has not gifted you as well.

Before we move on to the next chapter, I encourage you to take some time to quiet yourself and listen to God, dig into His Word and record what He thinks about you. (**Psalm 139**, **Matthew 10:29-31**, **Romans 8:38**, **Jeremiah 29:11** are great places to start).

From what you know of Him, do you think He compares you to anyone else? Record your findings and your thoughts here:

_____
_____
_____
_____
_____
_____
_____
_____

Whenever I am not sure how my Heavenly Father feels about me; if he's stacking me up against another one of His daughters and disappointed that I'm not measuring up, I remember the parable of the lost sheep. (**Luke 15:1-7**). My Father loves me individually, and never will leave me behind. I am that 1 sheep. When you're feeling lost, remind yourself of this too.

God isn't looking in your mirror, wishing you were someone else. He has eyes only for you. Another woman's looks, abilities, book smarts, family upbringing, position… none of that will ever negate your special, unique and beautiful qualities, and the specific goals God has planned for you. Do not look to the left or right. Be a giant, living in your Promised Land.

> *"For I know the plans I have for you, declares the Lord, plans to prosper you and not to harm you, plans to give you hope and a future!"* ~ **Jeremiah 29:11**

Session 3

Spoiler # 5 - Competition

Get Into It

I live in a house full of men. I'm completely outnumbered. There's a hefty amount of testosterone surrounding me, and when we play games together, the competition is real. I always suggest playing a game with good intentions of bringing the family together and have a picture in my mind of my happy little crew giggling and playing Monopoly or UNO together. The reality is that, without fail, there will often be pouting, pushing, screaming, and perhaps even some game pieces being whipped violently on the floor in protest to a loss. All the while, the winner is smugly rubbing in their victory. Yup. That's my boys.

I am guessing that you may have been able to picture that scene in your head because you too have witnessed children unable to keep it together when they experience the disappointment and dissatisfaction of being beat. It's silly and childish, right?

> Girls aren't always made of sugar and spice and everything nice.

And yet, if we're honest, although we might be able to play it cool on the exterior, we have all probably at some point been reduced to feeling that way on the inside, even if we aren't revealing it to anyone.

Girls aren't always made of sugar and spice and everything nice. We fiercely compete. There's often something inside of us that wants to win the coveted spot of most well liked, most beautiful, best mother award, or most Pinterest perfect house.

If we dig down deep and search our motives, our pride, and that drive to be on top, fuels much of our decision making. And yet, being on top is the complete opposite location we found Jesus, our example for righteous living.

Get Insight

My kids love to gloat. It is their first natural instinct to revel in their success and remind others of it. We do our best to teach humility, but they are not quite at the maturity level where they can purely celebrate others success if it meant their defeat.

> Making it known that you've got an edge will always drive a wedge.

Just the other day my eldest son came home from his baseball game absolutely elated that he had struck out everyone on the opposing team - including some of his friends. I reminded him that it would not be in his best interest to remind them about his victory on Monday at school.

Gloating is unbecoming, ladies, and it is sure to separate us. Our "gloating" may come in different, more subtle forms than our children's, but it is still divisive. A proud post on social media about our possessions and accomplishments, or slipping some information into a conversation that may puff us up are all elusive forms of gloating, but they are definite relationship killers.

So, I will repeat - enjoying, and making it known that you've got an edge will always drive a wedge.

Session 3

Get Inspiration

Gloating and a competitive nature will not only not sit well with others, it certainly does not sit well with The Lord. Write down how **Proverbs 24:17-18** says God handles gloaters:

_____
_____
_____

Gloating is acting superior about what has been, but boasting is acting superior about what is to come. Read what **James 4:13-17** has to say about boasting. Write down verse 16 here:

_____
_____
_____

My version uses strong language concerning boasting. It says that we boast out of "arrogance", and that boasting is "evil". Keeping these words in mind will help us hold back when we are tempted to boast.

We must also keep in mind who we are to be impressing and pleasing. Write down **Colossians 3:23** here

_____
_____
_____

From the moment Jesus made His not so grand entrance on our Earth's soil, to his final taxing, exhausted, broken hearted breath, He came to serve.

The Get Along Guide

Jot down **Mark 10:45** here _____
_____
_____

What does God tell us about how we should view potential "contenders"?

Matthew 19:30 _____
_____
_____

Philippians 2:3-4 _____
_____
_____

How can we possibly put others before ourselves, or think of them as more important, if we are striving to get ahead of them? We simply cannot. Competition will continually drive wedges between you and others, because no one enjoys being around another woman who makes her feel like a loser.

So, when you are tempted to think that you will win the admiration of another woman via superiority, remember that you will more likely succeed in winning her disdain and contempt. Even worse, you could make her feel less-than. So, remember: your edge will always drive a wedge.

Get Intentional

What are some things that we can do to avoid competition and encourage camaraderie?

Romans 12:15 is the Biblical response of how to respond when others fail, and when they succeed. Write it down here:

_____
_____
_____
_____

Now, jot down **Galatians 6:4**

_____
_____
_____
_____

Paul is instructing us here to rate ourselves against *ourselves*, rather than comparing and competing with our neighbor. Some translations use the word "boast" for testing ourselves, which seems contrary to what we've been discussing, but Paul isn't instructing us to brag, rather to weigh and evaluate ourselves honestly.

Who in your life do you feel urges to compete with? Whose life are you stacking up against yours? Who have you been guilty of gloating or boasting covertly to?

_____
_____
_____
_____

When we live and work to please God and focus on Him, and not to compete against another or win their affection or approval, competition dies. But, if your motivation is to impress or beat out others, they become your masters and rule over you.

It is ok to want to succeed, but when aiming high, it is much healthier to develop a "personal best" mentality rather than a "stomp on the rest" mentality. Relationship *always* trumps rank!

Remember that there is room enough for us all! God's great big world is vast enough to hold the beauty, talent and knowledge of both you and her. Just because she is succeeding, doesn't make you a loser. When we're focusing on living out God's specific call for us, we all win!

> *"Do nothing out of selfish ambition or vain conceit. Rather, in humility value others above yourselves, not looking to your own interests but each of you to the interests of others."* ~ **Philippians 2:3-4**

Spoiler # 6 - Insecurity

Get Into It

Insecurity (fear) is often the root of all the relentless weeds of judgement, pride, jealousy, envy, and comparing ourselves to one another. It's hold is tight, keeping us from reaching out to others and experiencing true intimacy.

Insecurities can be perceived as more of an inward battle, but they nonetheless, come between you and others. They cause us to obsess about ourselves and think poorly of others. As Carey Nieuwof puts it, in his book *Didn't See It Coming*, "Because you feel bad about yourself, you can't feel good about others. Once again, insecurity has led you to *focus on yourself to the exclusion of others."* 4

You won't see it coming, but insecurity will keep you from championing the women around you, drive a wedge between you and others, and ultimately isolate you. This is why we need to deal with our insecurities head on.

I urge you to read Beth Moore's book, *So Long Insecurity: You've been a bad friend to us!* It helped me pinpoint my own areas of insecurity and why they have reared their ugly head in the first place. Understanding the "why" of my insecurities really helps me spar against them as they begin to surface.

Get Insight

Many of our insecurities are birthed during childhood. During these formative years, our experiences, what people have done or said to us, traumatic or life altering events...all of these shape our insecurities.

There also can be distinctive moments in our adult life that contribute to our insecurities as well. Rejections like divorce or a job loss, the death of a loved one and even something as simple as an embarrassment may yank the carpet from underneath us, threatening our firm footing.

> Insecurity makes us uncertain about God as well as ourselves.

In *Why Can't We all Just Get Along!?*, I share how, as a young woman, I chronically compared myself to another woman. I concluded that I did not measure up. I cultivated and nurtured that "grasshopper" mentality. It snowballed into jealousy, self pity and yes, hatred. This was because I believed Satan's lies about distressing events in my past, and had not yet fully believed who God said I was.

The dictionary defines insecurity as an uncertainty about one's self. I would suggest that insecurity makes us uncertain about God as well - about His goodness and His capability. If that's you, I believe that the Lord wants to give you a new revelation today, which will empower you to combat and conquer those fears and become a confident, sure footed woman. I'd be honored to help you connect the dots.

Let's look back, so that we can move forward.

Lord, I pray for wisdom, clarity of thought and divine revelation for each and every incredibly brave woman who attempts to get to the bottom of her insecurities. Thank you Lord, that you are our safe place and that you cover over us with your feathers and shelter us with your wings (**Psalm 91:4**).

Get Inspiration

Before we look backward and inward, let's look upward. God's Word will always tell us more truth about us than anyone else, including ourselves.

Look up **Ephesians 2:10** and write down in capital letters what adjective is used to describe you here: _____

_____
_____

You may have written down the words "Workmanship", "Handiwork", or (my favorite) "Masterpiece".

Ladies, this is how God views you - and God knows best. How you view yourself will never be as accurate as your all knowing, loving Creator.

Later on in this study you will learn more on the truth about you.

Psalm 18:33 and **Habakkuk 3:19** both say that He makes us as sure footed as the _____.

Really!? A deer? It is definitely not the first image that comes to mind when I think of "fierce". They aren't quite the "king of the jungle" type animals we would assume could be sure of themselves. Fierce they may not be, but sure footed, yes.

Many deer roam my backyard. Sometimes they dart off, but often we can inch closer and closer without them flinching. Deer are known to walk with head held high, even in the rockiest of places. They rarely stumble, even through daunting terrain. My version of **Psalm 18:33** says "He set me secure on the heights". This tells me that God can help us walk, head held high, even in the rockiest of situations. May we lift our heads as well, trusting God along the way.

> You can trust God to be in the driver's seat of your life.

If you've been in church as long as I have, you might have the familiar tune flooding into your head "As the deer pants for the waters...". David asked the Lord to make him thirst for God the way a deer thirsts for water. Do not mistake this as a sign of weakness. It is one of strength because when we are weak, He is strong for us. You may feel weak and insecure, but as you become entirely dependent on Christ, His strength will be more than you ever need.

Write down **Psalm 40:2** here: _____
_____
_____
_____

What God did for David, He can do for you. He can pull you out of your destructive thoughts and the miry bog of negative beliefs you carry about yourself and set your feet upon a rock, making your steps secure.

Remember that he created you purposefully and perfectly. What does **Philippians 1:6** promise us? _____
_____
_____

God is not done with you yet. You are a work in progress, but you are being made whole. He has great plans for you - to bless you and not to harm you. You can trust God to be in the driver's seat of your life. Be confident in that.

Get Intentional

We are going to linger in this section longer than the other chapters, because I want you to dig a little deeper here.

This will be hard. But, I know that you are brave and seeking transformation.

Write down the areas of your past that may have been difficult, traumatic or were life altering events for you:

_____
_____
_____
_____

What are the areas where you feel insecure today?

Do you see a connection between those events and the events listed above? What is the common thread?

Now pray. Ask God to give you new revelation to pinpoint the origin of your insecurity so that you may begin your journey towards confidence. How is God speaking to you?

_____
_____
_____
_____
_____
_____
_____

We reside in a broken world. We were raised by broken parents. We are loved and hurt by broken people. We have been wronged by people who have been wronged by others. And, the enemy wants us to remain broken. BUT...

Isaiah 54:17

Write it down.
Speak it out loud.
Memorize it.
Believe it.
It's true.

_____
_____
_____
_____

Ladies, NO weapon formed against us will prosper. You can refute every tongue that is against you. When the enemy tells you that you are not worthy, that nothing will change, that you were just born like this, you'll always have to deal with this, that you don't measure up and that you'd be better off alone, silent, dead....THIS is when you quickly tell him that his dirty lies won't work anymore. Light penetrates darkness - not the other way around! And when you want to tell yourself these lies, remember that God's view of you is much more true!

Instead, this:

Psalm 139:14

Write it down.
Speak it out loud.
Memorize it.
Believe it.
It's true

_____
_____
_____
_____
_____
_____

That's right. Your life was not an accident, you aren't a failure or insignificant, ugly or unseen. You haven't screwed up one too many times for God to write you off. You were made on purpose for a great purpose and teamed up with your maker, you've got this.

I encourage you to take the time to read the entirety of **Psalm 139**. What truth about you have you never believed or may have forgotten?

The Get Along Guide

What one of God's messages has been muddled by the media?

_____
_____
_____
_____

The real truth is that God made you *perfectly*. Although this life has chipped away, cracked and beveled the parts that should have been smooth, God is ready and able to put the pieces back together. He thinks about you continually. He wants to build you up again. He is your source of strength and confidence. And, as you begin to truly believe that and cheer yourself on, you will then begin to cheer on those around you.

> *She is clothed with strength and dignity, she laughs without fear of the future."* ~ **Proverbs 31:25**

Session 4

Spoiler # 7 - Misunderstandings (and our own heads)

Get Into It

The mind is a wild place. Sometimes we can be our own worst enemy. Just think - how many times have you replayed scenarios, over analyzed conversations or questioned intentions? And, in the digital age we live in, misunderstandings are that much more prevalent. Text messaging alone is one of the biggest offenders. It is hard to read between the lines of text. We often try and we often fail.

We must remain fully aware that Satan uses anything he can get his hands on - the pitfalls of technology, confusion, distortion, miscommunication and our own wild imaginations, to blow things out of proportion and cause division among us. If there was a New York Times best selling book on lies, guess who the author would be.

Get Insight

Most of our battles with others go no further than our brains. We may not ever belittle, confront, accuse or engage in conflict with another woman face to face, but we certainly may have a showdown with her in our thought life. I am willing to bet my favorite uncle that you have carried on less than lovely conversations with another woman inside your head, and they have escalated far beyond what you'd ever let them in "real" life. The problem is that our thought life contributes to our entire lives. As Pastor Craig Groeschel says, "our lives are moving in the direction of our strongest thoughts". And so, if we allow negativity and untruths about others to linger inside our brains, it will eventually seep out.

> If we allow negativity and untruths about others to linger in our brains, it will eventually seep out.

Lysa Terkeurst illustrates how our mind can drag us into wild places and drive wedges between us in her book *Uninvited*. In the chapter entitled "There's a lady at the gym who hates me" Lysa candidly shares how she allowed her mind to wander about the woman working out beside her:

> *"Conjure up a picture in your mind of the most athletic person you know. The one who doesn't have a drop of fat on her entire body, not even at her belly button, which should be illegal in my cellulite-ridden opinion. Ok, do you have your person? That's her. She's honestly stunningly beautiful. Then picture a marshmallow dressed in a T-shirt and spandex pants. Her ponytail is rather tight, but not much else is. That's me. Hello world. So, I had to sort of get in her space just a tad to mount my machine, and I think I threw off her rhythm. That was sin number one....and then I tried to stay in sync with her...That was sin number two. And then there may have been a little issue with me taking a phone call while working out...I tried to talk quietly, but when you feel like a lung might very well pop out of your mouth, it's difficult to whisper-talk. That was sin number three. Three strikes, and she deemed me out. Out of my mind. Out of line. Out of control. She abandoned her elliptical and moved over to the treadmill. And she's hated me ever since."* [5]

Once Lysa came to her senses though, she rewrote the narrative in her head to what she believes the story actually was:

> *"There's a lady at the gym who really enjoys her workouts. One day the gal next to her talked on the phone, so instead of making a big deal out of it, she just transitioned over to the treadmill. She really hadn't thought of it much since."*

End of story.

Lysa's mountain was reduced to a molehill because she decided to change the narrative in her head and seek out truth. She realized that what we believe about a person may be a big, fat, cellulite-ridden lie.

Get Inspiration

The progression of sin - all deceptive, destructive and selfish desires are birthed in the heart. The heart then tries to convince the mind to harbor thoughts that open the door to express these sinful ambitions.

> What we believe about a person may be a big, fat, cellulite-ridden lie.

If the heart can win over the mind, we may choose to act on these thoughts, causing damage somewhere. This is why we are challenged to "be transformed by the renewing of our minds," and to "take every thought captive to the obedience of Christ." We battle in our minds so we can tame the heart.

James 1:15 tells us that when our evil desires are conceived they give birth to sin. And, when sin is fully grown it gives birth to death. Our inner thoughts, invisible as they are, are enough to defile us (**Mark 7:2–23**). Satan cannot control our minds, but he definitely can influence our thoughts - and he does. He knows that our unchecked sinful thoughts evolve into sinful deeds. God tells us though, how to nip sinful thoughts in the bud.

Record **2 Corinthians 10:5** _____
_____
_____
_____

Paul is using language his readers would be familiar with. In that time, when Rome conquered a city, the soldiers would chain up the leaders of that town and triumphantly parade them behind the soldiers as a statement to the public that they had been subdued. Paul was challenging them, and now us, to do that with our thoughts - to chain them down and force them to march behind us, rather than lead the charge.

God has given us power over our own minds to bring it into submission to Him. He will not allow you to endure any temptation which you cannot bear. He has provided the tools to help us do this. There is always a way to change your mind. This is what you can do:

Make note of **Philippians 4:8** _____
_____
_____
_____

When negative thoughts creep in, replace them with positive ones. Our minds remember patterns that we forge and will, in due course, travel there automatically. We simply need to tame the wild beast, and retrain one thought at a time. Just ahead of verse 8, **Philippians 4:6-7** tells us that prayer is another active ingredient in tamed thoughts, and as a result peaceful ones! Peaceful minds help achieve peaceful relationships. I encourage you to spend more time talking and listening to God than reciting and replaying your own words over in your head.

Sometimes I struggle with being positive and level headed. My thoughts can be easily swayed by emotion. I can be painfully over analytical. If you're the same, meditate on these verses for a while.

2 Timothy 1:7 _____
_____
_____
_____

Isaiah 26:3 _____
_____
_____
_____

God has gifted us the ability to have a sensible, balanced, healthy and sound mind - not an irrational one. We can remain in a state of perfect peace when our minds stay on Christ.

> Peaceful minds help acheive peaceful relationships.

Sounds Idyllic, right? Perfect peace. When we can fix our mind (who's doesn't need fixing?), control our thoughts (they often need taming) and think about the right things (because we are prone to wander to the wrong ones), we not only enjoy peace within ourselves, but peace with one another.

1 Corinthians 14:33 says that God is not a God of confusion, but he's a God of peace. He is the Prince of Peace! That means that He offers peace to whoever will dwell in His precinct. That's the zip code I want to live in!

I pray that this helps you fix your thoughts on Christ, so they can be made obedient to Him. I am confident it will be helpful to you in your interactions with others.

Get Intentional

In *Why Can't We All Just Get Along?!* (pg 70), my friend Laura shares how she got stuck listening to The Enemy's lies and her own false beliefs about herself - that women hate her. She realized that the only way to tune out those voices is to listen closely to the words of her Father.

Record a time when you have fallen prey to listening to:

The liar: _____

_____

_____

Yourself: _____

_____

_____

And now, record what you now know to be the truth, and what God says about it:

Your Heavenly Father: _____

Session 4

_____
_____
_____
_____

Before we conclude this section, we are going to take a quick look at one interesting and surprising way I've discovered to safeguard ourselves against Satan. Look up this one last scripture regarding your mind. It may come out of left field for you, but it's important that you grasp its power and effectiveness against the author of lies.

Read **2 Corinthians 2:10 b-11** - Take notice of the subject Paul is writing on here from the subtitle, and then write down verse 11.

_____
_____
_____
_____

Wow. Forgiveness is used as a tool against the enemy's trickery. Wouldn't you know it - next we will be exploring how to truly forgive.

> *"Whatever is true, noble, right, pure, lovely, admirable, excellent or praiseworthy - think about those things."*
> **Philippians 4:8**

Spoiler # 8 - Unforgiveness

Get Into It

What a huge, heavy subject to tackle. We all have had reason and need to forgive someone. Thankfully, we are also all recipients of God's forgiveness. Nonetheless, we must dive in and take a look at the Lord's opinion on holding grudges and carrying an offense towards another woman. We're going to "get into it" in God's word

Get Insight

In my studies and experience, I've discovered four ways that unforgiveness can be overcome. We are going to journey through them soon.

First, turn to the front of your Bible to **Genesis 45:1-15**. If you know anything about the story of Joseph, you know he had every earthly right to be consumed with rage and punish his brothers for what they did to him. Yet, read on to see how he treated them.

> Unforgiveness clogs the arteries between us and the heart of God.

In *Why Can't We All Just Get Along!?*, we discuss the Greek words that describe the word forgiveness - Charizomai, which means "to give grace" and "Aphiemi", which means "to send away" or "to let go". Aside from Jesus, I cannot think of any other Biblical example of offering grace to an offender and "letting go" than Joseph. I imagine that it wasn't an obvious or easy journey for Joseph to be in a place where he could fully forgive his brothers, and I am certain he would have had to practice the following four "R's" over and over.

Session 4

Before we look at those concepts, look up these startling verses and record your findings....

Mark 11:25: _____

_____

_____

_____

_____

Matt 6:14, 15: _____

_____

_____

_____

_____

Evidently, there is a lot at stake here, when we refuse to offer grace and hold on tight to our hurts. Forgiveness is nowhere near a straightforward journey. Many of us want to forgive, but do not know how to go about it. Let me offer you some guidelines that I have discovered are helpful in reaching that glorious destination.

Get Inspiration

In Genesis 45, we see the benefits for all involved, when Joseph clearly took the path, step by step, of forgiveness. In this chapter we see evidence of him releasing his right to use his position to punish his brothers, and instead he provides for them (v 11). He resists rage, and replaces it with an affectionate embrace (v 14,15). And, I'm certain that, as time went on, he resolved to revisit his choice to forgive, as he brought his family close to him in Egypt.

Let's learn to follow the footsteps of Joseph, leading us into the fullness of forgiveness...

#1 - Repair with resignation- When we resign we give up a position. In this case, we are handing over our rights as victims; fully aware that we have also been a victimizer at some point. We must give into our "right" to hold on to offense, realizing that we have already been forgiven much.

So, we must also actively repair what is broken by choosing to forgive. If we forgive others, God will also continually forgive us. Unforgiveness clogs the arteries between us and the heart of God.

Read **Ephesians 4:32** and write it down here -

_____
_____
_____
_____

Christ resigned His position of power to forgive, restore and repair our relationship with Him. We are to follow His lead.

#2 Refuse rage - Look back a few verses and jot down **Ephesians 4:26 - 27**.

_____
_____
_____
_____

Anger gives the enemy a "foothold" (a secure position from where further progress can be made). Essentially, an advantage or "one up". Instead, as the verse above instructs, we must be kind, tenderhearted and forgiving towards others.

Holding onto a grudge will only cause you grief, make you grumpy, bitter, and harden your heart over time. The devil absolutely prefers your heart to be a cold and hard one. A bitter heart never leads you to good things, and you can rarely trust your tongue when your heart is in that state. Remember that it is the warmth of God's kindness that leads us all to repentance.

#3 - Resist revenge - Do not rejoice when your enemy falls, or else the Lord will turn his anger away from them. Often, our unforgiveness embitters our hearts, making it difficult for others to be compassionate towards us. Also, when we seek out revenge, we trade our position of a clean-handed victim for a red-handed agressor - making us no better.

Write **Proverbs 24:17,18** down here:

_____
_____
_____
_____

#4 - Resolve and re-visit.

Record what **Hebrews 12:14** says:

_____
_____
_____

Striving indicates effort. Forgiveness is far from effortless, and it's not a "one and done" type thing.

It involves struggle and sheer determination. It is a continual act of the will - a training of the heart and mind. It's an ongoing decision we must make in order to properly love - remember 1 Corinthians 13, which states that love keeps no record of wrongs.

> Right feelings follow right actions.

Our natural feelings will buck against living at peace with someone who has offended or hurt us, but we must consciously work at it until our heart comes in line with our actions. Remember that *right feelings follow right actions*. The end result will be peace and righteousness.

I have certainly struggled my way through forgiveness. I've held on tight to what I thought were my rights. I've laid in bed, night after night, replaying in my mind how I could seek justice on my own terms and revenge. Yes, I've wished ill to come to my offender, although it makes me cringe to admit.

When I've come to my senses, I've prayed the Lord would free me, and He has. These biblical truths have been the key to unlocking the door to an enlarged, "wide open" future where I am experiencing the freedom of forgiveness. Unforgiveness truly does imprison you.

I find that #4 (Resolve and re-visit) has been a necessary part of my journey, as sin likes to creep up on us over and over again, just when we thought we were done with it. Thankfully, I've experienced the beauty of true and total forgiveness, and praise God that He "resolves and re-visits" me over and over again.

One thing I have found - God will take care of it. I want to dig in a bit on the area of revenge. Yes, we must resist it, but in my experience, this

Session 4

seems to be the most arduous aspect of forgiveness.

Look up what God says about how to handle revenge, and jot down:

Psalm 18:47 _____

_____

_____

_____

Romans 12:17 _____

_____

_____

_____

Matt 5:38-45 _____

_____

_____

_____

Proverbs 25:21 _____

_____

_____

_____

This world fights for justice. It's blasted in full view in every movie we take in. We want to see the bad guys go down. We rejoice when people who do evil are repaid with evil. However, God says that He will pay back those who harm us, and not to pay back evil with evil. He says it's our job to turn the other cheek, and actually bless our enemies. This is grace. I love what I heard Sheila Walsh says about this:

*"Grace is the antithesis of karma. We get what we **don't** deserve."*

Get Intentional

Who can I extend grace to today? _____

_____

Who do I need to repair things with? What relationship is broken (if even just a few cracks)?

_____

_____

What issues/feelings do I need to revisit and make certain are right?

_____

_____

How can I trust God with taking care of the things I want to deal with on my own? _____

_____

_____

Finally, one exersize that has helped me along in the forgiveness process is to use a passage of scripture I've already discussed, **Philippians 4:8**, as a guide to have better thoughts regarding my

Session 4

offender. This is what the passage instructs us to do:

> *"Finally, (sisters), whatever is true, whatever is honorable, whatever is right, whatever is pure, whatever is lovely, whatever is admirable, if there is anything excellent or praiseworthy, think on these things."*

I write a list of all the positive attributes I am instructed to think about and create a list of the good things I know about the person who offended me. After all, no one is fully "a sinner or a saint". Most of us are aiming to do our best, but stumble along the way.

This exersise helps me replace my negative, wayward and distorted thoughts that my unforgiveness has created and built up about my offender. It helps me see them in a new light, because what we focus on grows. When we dwell on bad things we will find bad things, but when we look for the good, we find the good. This is an incredibly powerful tool to help you begin to see and think more clearly about your offender, so I'd encourage you to give it a try. I challenge you to fill in as many blanks as you can.

> When we dwell on bad things we will find bad things, but when we look for the good, we find the good.

- True _____
- Honorable _____
- Right _____
- Pure _____
- Lovely _____
- Admirable _____
- Excellent _____

- Praiseworthy _____

As we do our best, God will do the rest. We must trust that He will work all things out for our good and His glory, and in the meantime, we extend grace and seek to remain at peace - *even* with our offenders.

I highly recommend the book *Total Forgiveness* by R.T. Kendall if you are seeking to completely forgive someone who has wronged you. Add this title to your list of must reads!

Thank you, ladies, for digging deep with me. It is not easy to be blatantly and brutally honest, and get real with God and ourselves.

Now that we've thrown the spoilers in the trash, we will begin to gather the good ingredients that will whip up sweet and healthy relationships. In his word, God has shown us how we should view ourselves, and how we should treat one another, so we can "get along" for our good and His glory.

SECTION 2

GOD'S RECIPE FOR SUCCESS IN YOUR RELATIONSHIPS

Session 5

Ingredient #1 - A Pinch of Patience

"Patience is bitter, but its fruit is sweet."~ Aristotle

Get Into It

I'm sitting at a red light, and this car pulls up beside me. I see a man and woman going at it, yelling and screaming at each other in total and complete rage. As the light turns green and they take off, I notice their bumper was plastered with stickers that (ironically) said "GOOD VIBES ONLY".

I chuckled a bit, but my first reaction was to scoff and roll my eyes. But then, I thought about the times I've screwed up, and not "practiced what I preached" too. My words, actions and attitudes haven't always matched my "bumper sticker". Despite the fact that I try, I'm lightyears from perfection.

> God is always patient with us, and we can learn to get it right more often.

Today we're diving into having patience with one another. Our central scripture, **Colossians 3:13-15** talks about making allowance for other's faults, because God has made allowance for ours. Remember that we're all reaching for "good vibes only", but sometimes we screw up. We aren't villains or hypocrites - we're all just human.

Ephesians 4:2 instructs us to "Always be humble and gentle. Be patient with each other, making allowance for each other's faults because of your love." This is the kind of patience we're talking about today. That word "always" trips me up every time. Truth is, like the couple in the car, we won't always be humble and gentle, making allowance for each other. The good news is that God is always patient with us, and we can learn to get it right more often.

Get Insight

Making allowance for another woman's faults is one thing. Offering grace when she has specifically sinned against you is another. Our last chapter tackled the difficult process of genuine forgiveness. There are times we need to dive head into a forgiveness journey, but most often, what we really just need with one another is pure patience. Patience is a vehicle that can steer you clear from needing to ask for forgiveness and will drive you directly to the land of "good vibes only".

> Patience is a vehicle that can steer you clear from needing to ask for forgiveness and will drive you directly to the land of "good vibes only".

What one of us doesn't need or want more patience in our lives? But, the reality is that what we want and need isn't always what we practice. My husband, a professional musician, often tells others that he instructs; "practice doesn't make perfect - practice makes permanent."

You see, if my son was to practice the wrong four chords on the piano over and over again, he wouldn't learn the song perfectly, would he? Instead, he would solidify those wrong chords in his head, making the song sound wrong and unpleasant. Practicing the wrong thing didn't make the song perfect - it simply solidified the wrong. We need to be careful to practice the *right* things in life, so they become more permanent fixtures.

The "good" news is that life, and others, will give us plenty of practice and opportunity to achieve a more permanent state of patience. The question is, will we respond the correct way?

Patience is never our initial go-to guttural reaction, when others' words, attitudes and actions aren't jiving with us.

It seems as though nearly everything that God commands us to do is counter to our own natural selfish inclinations. He is the King of a kingdom that seems upside down to us sometimes. God is counter culture.

> God's word has proven to be not only trustworthy, but so incredibly smart.

Loving our enemies and being kind to those who irritate us isn't always line one on our to-do list. Nonetheless, I know beyond a shadow of a doubt that God's word has proven to be not only trustworthy, but so incredibly smart. His ways are higher and better. He knows that patience yields miraculous results.

Let's look to God's word to become inspired towards patience.

Get Inspiration

Of course, if we want some inspiration, we ultimately should look to Jesus. We will do that in just one moment.

First, let's hear from a wise man (Solomon) who has offered generations of people sound, sage advice on the profit of practicing patience. For each of these verses, record the drawbacks of impatience, and the benefits of showing restraint:

The Get Along Guide

Proverbs 12:16 _____
_____
_____

Proverbs 15:1 _____
_____
_____

Proverbs 15:18 _____
_____
_____

Proverbs 17:14 _____
_____
_____

Proverbs 19:11 _____
_____
_____

Proverbs 21:23 _____
_____
_____

Clearly, there is much to be gained by practicing patience.

Now, take a look at this passage of scripture to see how Jesus, our go-to guy, handled difficult people and a difficult situation.

Look up **John 8:6-11** - How did Jesus respond to both the Pharisees (who, no doubt were provoking him) and the sinful woman (who had sinned against Him)?

_____
_____
_____
_____

Jesus handled them both beautifully. He remained calm, and He did not condemn. Yet, he was still able to "prove His point".

Now check out how Jesus responds to his disciples (and friends) in **Matthew 16:8-11** and **Luke 9:40-41**. I think we'd agree that we can feel his annoyance level rising, yet his words and actions show no signs of belittling, bashing or of Jesus losing his cool.

This happens throughout the New Testament. I can only imagine how much restraint Jesus would have had to exercise while He interacted with very imperfect people during his time here on Earth.

Even his closest friends did not understand Him, questioned Him and sinned against Him. There would have been countless times He could have responded, "You absolute nincompoops! You will never learn! There's no hope for you - I'm done!"

Skip back to **Luke 23:32-39** - write down Jesus's words, in the midst of all that was being done to Him.

_____
_____
_____
_____

Even in the most painful moments of His life, Jesus chose to be patient with the ones who surrounded Him. He got that they simply didn't know. He understood their humanity.

Jesus understands our humanity, yet he calls us higher - to be like Him, with His supernatural assistance.

Now, turn the pages of your Bible to **1 Corinthians 13:4** - a familiar, and wonderful passage indeed. It describes the essence of Love, something we're all on the hunt for.

What is the very first descriptive word used for love? _____

_____

If we are to be loving towards other women, and if we want others to be inspired to love us, we must exercise *patience* with her. I know what you're saying "but how!? BUT HOW!?"

Now turn to **Galatians 5:22** - another familiar passage.

What is the evidence of the Holy Spirit working in our lives?

> Patience isn't just waiting. It's our attitude while we're waiting

Love, joy, peace, _____, kindness, goodness, faithfulness, gentleness and self-control.

This list is absolutely impossible to achieve without the "supernatural assistance" - the intervention of the Holy Spirit. It is like running a marathon in high heels - not going to happen, sister. The Holy Spirit is our helper; like a nicely broken-in pair of Nike runners, helping us cross the finish line.

Romans 8:26 reassures us that the Holy Spirit helps us in our weakness, and **John 14:26** reminds us that He will teach us and remind us of everything that Jesus has told us.

Go underline those scriptures, write them down on note cards or in your journal - plaster them where you know you'll encounter them and run to them every time you feel weak on your own and need His supernatural assistance.

Before we get intentional, let's be inspired and challenged one more time by the words of Paul in **1 Corinthians 3:13-15**. Read the verses and then jot down how you are supposed to respond to other's faults.

_____
_____
_____
_____

What is the reason we are to respond that way? (V 13 b)

_____
_____

Now, record **Colossians 3:13** here: _____

_____
_____
_____

Patience isn't just waiting - it's our attitude *while* we're waiting. Do we hold our tongue, or do we spout off? Do we sigh, grunt and groan, or give it to God? The understanding of **Colossians 3:13** should give us a

God-sized attitude adjustment.

Recognizing that we've needed others to wait for us to get things right, will help us be patient while others are doing the same. We will have hearts of compassion, kindness and humility while we wait for others to get things right.

Paul says to "put on" love and "let" the peace of Christ rule. These are action words, reminding us again, that patience won't come naturally ("flip my lid" moments are what comes natural). We must strive for it …we must *practice* it.

> We ask you, Holy Spirit, to help us cover over the sins of others, and in doing so, display your love.

Get Intentional

It's practice time.

First of all, we pause now, and ask you, Holy Spirit to be with us and help us in the area of patience. Wrap around us, like a string on our finger; reminding us to extend grace, especially to the women who need it most. Thank you for covering over a multitude of our sins. We ask you, Holy Spirit, to help us cover over the sins of others, and in doing so, display your love.

Who in your household, workplace, the church pews that surround you, your community, needs you to practice patience with them? Jot down their names.

_____

_____

How can you exercise your patience muscles with them, the next time they begin to push your buttons? (Recall how Jesus handled others, and remember the Proverbs verses, and then apply those to your relationships and interactions)

___

Finally, write down the last time you recall someone else practicing patience with you. How did they respond to you, and how did that make you feel/respond back to them?

___

Trust me, when I tell you that I know what it's like to forebear with someone who feels like the embodiment of what Paul describes as a thorn in the flesh. My teeth have certainly gritted behind my smile.

Trust me, when I also say, that the thorn is there to make you more like a rose, soft and aromatic to others. And, you may absolutely view that thorn herself, as another rose one day too.

> *"Always be humble and gentle. Be patient with each other, making allowance for each other's faults because of your love."* **Ephesians 4:2**

Ingredient # 2 - A Cup of Confession

Get Into It

We just asked the Holy Spirit to help us cover over the offense of others, by being gracious and patient with them. In doing so, we display the love of Jesus. There is a time to conceal, or cover over sin, (**1 Peter 4:8**) but there is also a time to bring it to light.

"Confession" is a scary word. Most of us picture a dark booth with an intimidating spiritual figure on the other side of a curtain waiting for us to cough up our secrets.

Lately though, I've looked at confession as a much less scary thing, and here's why...

> When we reveal the improper choices we made yesterday, we shed light on our maturity today

Get Insight

There is good news about bringing our sin to light. When we reveal the improper choices we made yesterday, we shed light on our maturity today. While we cannot change our past, we can certainly learn from it, and handling our wrongdoing in the proper way certainly shows that we are learning and growing - and that's commendable.

Some people think that it's a sign of weakness to apologize and admit wrongdoing, but I say that "Sorry" is for the strong. Something I've learned over time is that it's even ok…and really helpful to say you're sorry, even when you aren't wrong, in order to mend a relationship that's been fractured. Relationship always trumps "rightness", so whether you are wrong or right, it's always right to apologize.

Get Inspiration

> Relationship always trumps "rightness"

Throughout scripture, we see that confession is crucial to us being restored to God. It is also crucial to us being restored, one to another. Let's look at a Biblical example of confession, and imagine the strength needed to muster an "I'm sorry".

Turn to **Luke 15:11-20**, and read the story that Jesus told.

Write down verses 18 and 19 here:

_____
_____
_____
_____
_____
_____

This boy's father was far enough removed to not know how his son was sinning against him. I imagine the son could have concealed what he had done, and how he was reduced to living. His sin, his pride or his fear of his father's reaction could have easily kept him away.

The Get Along Guide

Write down the entirety of **James 5:16**

_____
_____
_____
_____

Here we are again in a strenuous spot. Raise your hand if you enjoy divulging the shameful and embarrassing errors of your ways - to anybody. And, who of us allows the words "I'm sorry" to roll easily off their tongue? No one? I didn't think so.

Confession reveals weak moments and requires the servant position of an "I'm sorry". So, why would God lead us to such an uncomfortable place?

Look back at **James 5:16** in your Bible. What is the reason that we are to confess our sins to one another and pray for one another?

So that we may be _____.

That's right - so that we may be healed.

If you have an outstanding offense and a relationship that needs mending - whether the other individual realizes it or not, and you fear the end result of a confession - pay attention closely as we move on.

Now, write down the second half of verse 16.

_____
_____
_____
_____

The version I am using today says, "The earnest prayer of a righteous person has great power and wonderful results.

None of us are righteous, except because of Christ. When we prayerfully repent our wrongdoing to God, we are made righteous and we are ready to move on to better things. Not without making things right with others first. Another daunting step.

I can only imagine the fortitude and the brawn of humility it would have taken the son to face his father after he had selfishly and irresponsibly wasted His father's generous gift. He was putting himself at risk of rejection and punishment, yet he chose to return to his father and come clean - he chose to repent.

> The best way, the *only* way that we can mend broken relationships is to confess our sin and genuinely forgive one another.

What do verses 20 and 22 reveal about the posture of his father's heart, when he saw his "offender"? How does it say he responded to the boy's return?

_____
_____
_____
_____

The best way - the *only* way that we can mend broken relationships is to confess our sin and genuinely forgive one another - then move on.

That may mean that you are the instigator of a difficult conversation, and that's intimidating. It seems much easier to sweep our sin under the rug and forget it.

Our enemy wants us to let sin fester and remain hidden. Satan would much rather have an offense linger, spawning bitterness, hatred and hardened hearts. However, if we are to heed the instructions that James is giving us here, and hurl our heart junk and misdeeds out into the open, suddenly confusion, hurt and offense can be resolved.

I believe that when we have authentic hearts of repentance, pray and genuinely ask for forgiveness and fully "come clean", we will be welcomed back by God and we will be received well by others. And, who knows the wonderful results that will occur beyond that.

Get Intentional

Think back throughout your life. It make take a few moments. Is there someone who you have an outstanding offense with? Are you the offender? Are they? Whether it is you who is in the wrong, or another, **Matthew 18:15** gives clear instruction on what to do:

What does it say?

_____
_____
_____

Who should sins and offenses remain between?

_____
_____

That's right - you and her, and that's it. What does the verse say will happen if she hears you out?

_____
_____

Feel free to swap out the word "brother" for sister. You will gain a sister. Sisters, when in a healthy place, possess a loyalty that is unbreakable.

If you keep reading in **Matthew 18** you will see how to handle a situation if you and her just can't seem to work things through: "But if they will not listen, take one or two others along, so that "every matter may be established by the testimony of two or three witnesses."

I love how God's order is protective while being redemptive. If we walk His road to reconciliation we will be covered not only by Him, but others as well, and we will be released into freedom while doing it.

I have personally witnessed how direct conversation and deliberately seeking out forgiveness with the best of intentions in mind, has brought women closer together than before an offense. "I'm sorry - will you forgive me" are six very small words, but they resuscitate and reinforce relationships in a colossal way.

> "Sorry" is not only for the strong, but it makes us strong together.

Sorry is not only for the strong, but it makes us strong together.

I hope you now understand the benefits of confession, and are motivated to bring things to the light so that you are in right standing with God and with others.

When we confess our sin to one another and pray for one another, guess what!? Love grows.

"Love never fails" **1 Corinthians 3:8**

Session 6

Ingredient # 3 - An Ounce of Openness and a Teaspoon of Truth

Get Into It

In *"Why Can't We All Just Get Along?!"* (have you snatched that book up yet!?), I discuss the value of carrying one another's burdens. We cannot do that though, unless we first get real about our burdens and share them with one another.

We must be open about ourselves, but we must also be open and willing to enter other's imperfections with them. This is where I want to camp out in the "Get Inspiration" section of this chapter. Before we dig into God's Truth, let's dispel a lie.

Get Insight

Social media, girls, is not social - and it is definitely not real. You will never truly get to know your friends through a screen.

> You will never truly get to know your friends through a screen.

Openness and truth are necessary ingredients to any relationship. Unfortunately, the way our world is working these days, we are able to present our "highlight reel" to the ones around us via social media, and this is becoming the norm. Sadly, our "reel" friends can't become "real" friends.

What we present to others on our Facebook, Instagram, Snapchat or Tik Tok accounts is not the truth about us. Sure, it may be a more glossy, impressive us, but it's not who we authentically are.

In Scary Close, Donald Miller tells it like it is:

> *"It's true, people are attracted to intelligence and strength and even money, but attraction isn't intimacy. What attracts us doesn't always connect us."* [6]

> Will you save face, or will you let your guard down and live face to face?

So, the question I pose to you is, would you rather be envied or truly loved? What do you need more? Admiration, or intimacy? Will you save face, or will you let your guard down and live face to face?

It is nice to present a polished version of ourselves to the world, but I promise you, it is worlds better to be embraced for who we truly are - war wounds and all.

Jesus tells a story of two men who showed what can happen when we are open to others, in the midst of their mess, and when we reveal the truth of ourselves, so that we may be loved right where we're at.

Get Inspiration

Read through the Good Samaritan story in **Luke 10:30-37**.

To me, this is the true essence of bearing another's burden. I imagine the result would have been intimacy and loyalty between the two.

Record the actions of the "good samaritan" found in vs. 34 and 35.

My discoveries were these:

1. First he went over to him. He chose to leave his space and what he was focused on.
2. He then soothed his wounds. He risked his own comfort and got involved in his mess.
3. He put the man on a donkey and took him to an Inn and paid for his stay. He sacrificed his time and resources and even took a hit financially in order to help.

The Samaritan showed compassion and vulnerability. When you dress someone's wounds, not only are they in a vulnerable state, but you open yourself up to be vulnerable as well. I believe the result was mutual - they became invested in one another.

Now, let's talk about the truth.

> In relationships, truth is absolutely necessary.

Our truth is not always neat, nor is it noble. Sometimes it's nauseating. But, in relationships, truth is absolutely necessary.

It is easy for us to want to hide behind a mask of falsities that pretend we are someone different - even with our close friends. We resist airing our dirty laundry, for fear that the stench will keep others away. Truth is, we need the ones around us to lighten our load. This may mean that she may catch a whiff of that dirty laundry. I promise you though, the sweet aroma of true authentic friendship, overpowers the stench we feel we need to mask.

> The sweet aroma of true authentic friendship, overpowers the stench we feel we need to mask.

The Samaritan's truth was messy - and even dangerous. Imagine if he dragged himself to a more secluded place while he suffered. What if he wasn't in clear view for others to respond and help him in his time of need? I think we both know the grim answer to that question.

Perhaps you feel injured and vulnerable in some areas of your life - like damaged goods. If you continue to hide your hurt and conceal your cracks, I assure you that you will never be healed.

I've been learning about the "Belt of Truth" in a study I've been engaged in. Just like the Roman Soldier's belt provided him stability, resistance to injury, and a place for all his other protection to be anchored, the truth is the backbone of our relationships.

When we "drop the act", and allow others a front row seat to our lives, we allow ourselves to be truly known and therefore truly loved.

Write **John 8:32** here:

_____

_____

_____

The beautiful thing about the truth is that it truly sets us free. When we are able and willing to be open and honest about who we genuinely are, and embrace the women around us, we will experience liberty and love in our relationships like we've never known. Taking our guard down leads to holy ground.

Get Intentional

What can we learn from the story of The Good Samaritan about being open (like the Samaritan) and truthful about our situation (like the vulnerable, injured traveller)?

_____
_____
_____
_____

How can we be a "good Samaritan"; a good neighbor to another woman? Here are some ideas:

- Be available; not so caught up in your own life that you are oblivious or apathetic to the needs of others. Busyness is a compassion killer.
- Be willing to be involved in other women's messes and get messy yourself.
- Be open to sharing your story, your resources and your time.
- Make an investment in someone, and they will become more valuable to you. Where your treasure is, there your heart will be. **(Luke 12:34)**
- Be compassionate and humanize the other person.
- Be vulnerable and accessible - Don't try to have it all together. Personalize women, rather than looking at them like the competition. Realize they are just like you.

Can you think of any other ways? _____

_____
_____
_____
_____

Sometimes it's obvious that others need our help. The traveler who was helped by the Samaritan was clearly in distress. For most of us though, our troubles are easily bottled up and hidden behind smiles and screens. So, we must be careful not to be so absorbed in our own worlds that we miss a wounded woman. Even more, if we do recognize her need, we must never leave her on the side of the road.

Who in my world needs me to be her "good Samaritan? Who do I need to open myself up to?

_____
_____

What parts of my life do I need to let others see more of? How can it benefit me to be vulnerable?

_____
_____
_____
_____

> *"I imagine that the first question the priest and Levite asked was: 'If I stop to help this man, what will happen to me?' But by the very nature of his concern, the good Samaritan reversed the question: 'If I do not stop to help this man, what will happen to him?'"* [7]
> *~ Martin Luther King Jr., Strength to Love*

Ingredient # 4 - A Smidgeon of Service and a Liter of Love

Get Into It

I imagine the Samaritan's heart went out to the suffering man on the side of the road. Compassion and empathy were clearly present. The Samaritan would have put himself in his shoes, enabling him to reach out and do what he'd wish someone - anyone - would do for him in that situation.

And so, the Samaritan displayed love very practically. He practiced the Golden Rule:

> *"Do unto others as you would have them do unto you."*

The Golden Rule isn't just a sappy slogan that our mothers quoted when we weren't getting along - it is a command of Jesus (among the greatest commands) that has seeped out to mainstream culture as among the most noble, selfless actions we can take. It holds power when it is harnessed, and yet, it is easy to want to protect ourselves more than the feelings and needs of others.

> The Golden Rule isn't just a sappy slogan that our mothers quote when we weren't getting along.

Get Insight

Serving others probably isn't at the top of your to-do list. Mine either. Protecting the feelings, rights and needs of others above ourselves isn't an enticing thought. We should take careful thought of **Romans 14:13** though, and consider how this applies to serving the women around us.

Write the verse down here:

_____

_____

_____

_____

We often think that serving others involves bringing them something. We count on a waitress to bring us coffee, tea or something yummy to eat, but we also hope that she removes the sticky smudges from our table before we get our sleeves stuck too.

> "How can I encourage and build this woman up, rather than add a stumbling block in her life?"

Like a good wait staff, **Romans 14:13** challenges us to serve others by making sure we remove something potentially harmful from their life as well.

Catering to another woman's needs comes in many forms. When we remove stumbling blocks for her we are also serving her. This means considering her feelings, struggles and needs and then doing what we can to eliminate further struggle for her.

It is important to ask ourselves questions like, "How can I encourage and build this woman up, rather than add a stumbling block in her life?" This may go against the grain of our desire to make ourselves feel bigger or better, but it is the braver action, if we want to please the Lord and if we want healthy relationships.

When we consider ourselves only, we can often kick other women when they are down. When we boast about our accomplishments, we may diminish theirs in their own eyes. When we feel the need to "one up", we push her down.

Insensitivity is a compassion killer - and it's a relationship killer. The book that leads to life, however, teaches us how our relationships will come forth as gold by using The Golden Rule. Gold, as you know, is strong, beautiful and enduring.

Get Inspiration

Jot down **Galatians 5:14** _____

_____

_____

_____

_____

Read below a similar statement found in **Matthew 7:12** as recorded in my New Living Translation:

> *"Do to others whatever you would like them to do to you".*

And, I love what The Message translation adds:

> *"Here is a simple, rule-of-thumb guide for behavior: Ask yourself what you want people to do for you, then **grab the initiative** and do it for them. Add up God's Law and Prophets and this is what you get."*

The Message uses verbiage that I love - grab the initiative.

Let us not wait to do good for others, but take action and seek out moments and opportunities to bless others - yes, even the ones who persecute us.

What does **Mark 12:30-31** tell us?

_____
_____
_____
_____

He reminds us that loving others is right up there just after loving God.

What is one reason that **1 John 4:11-12** says why we should love each other?

_____
_____
_____

We are selfish by human nature. We want good things for ourselves first. We are concerned about our own interests and consumed with building our own earthly kingdoms.

But, when we refocus our energy, time, resources on loving others in action and doing for them what we hope for ourselves, we are fulfilling God's greatest command, and we are emulating Him. Now, this takes resolve; a decision - it won't come naturally.

Session 6

Get Intentional

Below is an area where you can brainstorm how you can love others as you love yourself.

Fill in briefly what these things are for YOU.

My hopes and dreams:

_____
_____
_____
_____

My interests:

_____
_____
_____
_____

My loves:

_____
_____
_____
_____

My needs:

_____
_____
_____

Think of another woman you know, and fill in what you think could be her answers in each area. If you don't know for sure, that's ok. Now, think about how you could be a blessing to her in each area. How can you aid in her fulfilling her dream? How could you give her opportunity to enjoy her interests? How can you bless the ones she loves (her children, parents, etc)? How can you meet a need of hers? How could you make her shine?

Her hopes and dreams:
_____
_____

A small way I could help or encourage her in these:
_____
_____

Her interests:
_____
_____

A small way I could help or encourage her in these:
_____
_____

Her loves:
_____
_____

A small way I could help or encourage her in these:

_____

_____

Her needs:

_____

_____

A small way I could help or encourage her in these:

_____

_____

Helping fill in the blanks in her life is love in action! It is taking the initiative that The Message translation is referring to in **Mark 12:3**.

I love the quote from Jacque Watkins that says *"Be the friend you long to have. Give one hundred percent. Give as you would want it given to you."* This is precisely what James is talking about below.

"Love your neighbor as yourself"
James 2:8

"If I then, your Lord and Teacher, have washed your feet, you also ought to wash one another's feet."
John 13:14

Session 7

Ingredient # 5 - A Dash of Discretion (James 4:11)

Get Into It

Our teeny tiny tongues are difficult to control and can get us in heaps of trouble. The most surefire way to keep from speaking out of line is not to speak at all! But, since many of us women have the gift of gab, we must filter filter filter!

Here's the first filter: keep your negative thoughts to yourself. I'm going to repeat that: keep your negative thoughts to yourself!

First, a filter prevents impurities from passing through. It blocks them from contaminating the useful parts you are attempting to preserve. When we block our impure thoughts from escaping our mouth, we become much more purposeful to others. The good parts of us are then ready to add health and positivity - something sweet to those who are experiencing us.

> A filter prevents impurities from passing through. It blocks them from contaminating the useful parts you are attempting to preserve.

Every so often I indulge and bake a delicious blueberry scone recipe. The thing that makes it really tasty and almost irresistible is it's lemon glaze made purely of lemon juice, butter and confectioners sugar. In order to achieve a perfectly smooth glaze, the instructions tell me to sift the sugar first. Why? The melted butter and lemon juice will not mix as well into the sugar if there are lumps. It would create unappetizing, dry, sour pockets in the glaze - something I'd want to spit out. But, when that sugar has first been sifted properly, everything goes down smoothly and sweetly. It is the same with our thoughts, words and actions. Sifting always smooths everything out.

You can dramatically influence and sour someone else's thoughts about another woman by even a slight unsifted, passing comment you make. There is power in the spoken word. You can curse or you can bless someone. I implore you to do the latter!

Here, we will focus not only on learning how and why to filter our words, but the necessity of fusing them with the truth of God's word.

Get Insight

I've unfortunately had to explain to my children that "hurt people hurt people". What I mean by that is, the ones who are bringing them down with their words - mocking, using sarcasm, spreading untruth - they are most likely doing so because they have been brought down themselves by someone else. They speak negatively because negativity has either been modeled to them or spoken over them.

> Hurt people hurt people.

The truth is though, that we will never feel bigger by belittling someone else. It is our job to break the negativity cycle. I promise that when we speak well of and to the women around us, others will see the best in us. Speaking life points others to the Life-Giver, and that is always our goal.

Get Inspiration

Look up these verses - they are God's instructions for that little, but mighty tongue of ours. What do they say?

Psalm 34:13 _____
_____
_____

James 1:26 _____
_____
_____

Proberbs 18:21 _____
_____
_____

The bible instructs to be slow and careful when using your tongue, and even sometimes not to use it at all:

According to **James 1:19**, we must be _____ to listen

and _____ to speak.

Proverbs 21:23 tells us that whoever keeps her tongue in control

keeps _____

The Get Along Guide

And, **Proverbs 17:28** says that even a _____ who keeps silent is considered _____

For the chatterboxes, this can be tricky. Heck, it can seem near impossible without divine intervention. Recently, my chatterbox son who had damaged his vocal chords could not even be bribed with cold hard cash to remain quiet. But, with the Lord, ALL things are possible! (I'm exhorting myself here!)

> Filter, filter, filter!

God knows our words can get us into trouble quickly, which is why he warns us to think before we speak. If we blurt out whatever comes to us, His word says that turmoil, anger and strife await.

As with all of God's ways, He is loving and protects us by steering (and sometimes yanking) us in the right direction. Sometimes I think I can hear him saying the same words to me that I said to you: "Danielle! Filter, filter, filter!".

Read these verses to realize how our words can lead us into problems that we could otherwise avoid.

2 Timothy 2:16 _____
_____
_____

Proverbs 16:28 _____
_____
_____

Proberbs 15:1 _____
_____
_____

Proverbs 17:9 _____
_____
_____

Who wants anger, strife, ungodliness and disunity in their life!? Not me! If you don't either, listen to the Lord as he reminds us to "filter filter filter!".

The Proverbs are packed with advice and instruction regarding our tongues.

Proverbs 21:23 assures us that if we "keep" our tongue, we will keep out of trouble. **Proverbs 12:18** says that instead, the tongue of the "wise" brings healing. And, **Proverbs 20:15** claims that wise speech is more valuable to us than gold and rubies. It would be sagacious of us to recognize the power that we have in communicating and speaking well with, about and to the women around us.

Get Intentional

It is time to take a moment and reflect on how our words are impacting others in our lives. Have you hurt or cursed another woman with your words? Have you knocked her down a peg with a sarcastic remark that was masked as a joke? Perhaps you have not "kept" your words to yourself, allowing venom to seep out of your tongue about her to others?

Take a moment to repent and ask the Lord to use your tongue to bless, and not make a mess.

Circle the areas you struggle the most with your words?

- Harsh words
- Lies and deceit
- Passive-Agressive comments
- Belittling
- Gossip
- Sarcasm
- Backhanded compliments
- Flattery
- Criticizing
- Other: _____

Jot down a prayer asking God to help you season your words with gentleness, truth, encouragement, grace and discretion.

_____
_____
_____
_____
_____

Lord, we ask, along with the Psalmist, for you to "watch over the door of my lips" (**Psalms 141:3**) so that we can become like the Proverbs 31 wife who "opens her mouth with wisdom" (**Proverbs 31:26**), and so that our mouths can be a "fountain of life" (**Proverbs 10:11**). A tree is known by its fruit. Our words reflect who we truly are.

"Out of the abundance of the heart the mouth speaks"
Matthew 12:34

Ingredient # 6 - Blend in Blessing (Romans 12:14)

Get Into It

"Right Feelings follow right actions." Remember this phrase? This is something I've come to realize is very true. When I make the right food choices, I have more energy. When I work out regularly, I feel stronger. When I choose to let a hurtful comment go, I'm suddenly released from it's hold on me. When I am a good friend to others, I find myself surrounded by good friends. I'm no longer lonely, but feeling loved.

All those good feelings I'm looking for don't come without me first making the right choice. I need to act the right way in order to benefit from it's result, which usually is accompanied by good feelings.

Our feelings should never be in the driver's seat of our lives, but it is certainly helpful to feel loving towards others. I would like to suggest that when we act lovingly towards them, we have a better chance of feeling love towards them and back from them. Even if not, we will know we've done the right thing.

> I need to act the right way in order to benefit from it's result.

I want you to keep this phrase in mind as we dive into the topic of blessing those who persecute us.

Get Insight

There are different "categories" of people who require us to have extra outside help in order to respond to them in an appropriate way. First, there are those who actually persecute us because of our faith in Christ. The second group are those who irritate us with their different personalities or fallen human nature. The third are people who may have offended us or mishandled our hearts either unintentionally or because of their toxic nature.

All forms of mistreatment are to be expected, because of our broken world. Jesus reminds us in **John 15:18-27** that the world hated Him, and so it is inevitable that the world will, at times, hate us too. It is wise to be prepared for friction. Thankfully, Christ has both instructed us on and set an example of how to handle each situation.

> We are never more Christlike than when we love people who can't, or don't, love us in return.

In **Ephesians 4:1-3**, Paul exhorts the church to walk with patience, bearing with one another in love and eager to maintain unity. This is how we are to handle those who rub us the wrong way. The rest of this chapter will instruct us on how to respond to those who have truly wronged us.

Our goal in life is Christlikeness. We are never more Christlike than when we love people who can't - or don't - love us in return. Think about the immensity and extent of Jesus' love for you. If you're reading this, I'm assuming you aim to love Him back. But, if you're anything like me, you don't, and you can't possibly display your love for Him like He deserves. In fact, there are times we outright forget Him; leave Him out of the equation, hurt Him and downright disobey. There are times we are numb and apathetic towards Him, and yet, He keeps on pursuing...keeps on loving....keeps on blessing.

There are others who've decided to make Christ their enemy. They reject and refuse His great love for them. Some are still simply unaware. Christ keeps on loving every single one of us. And, He is calling us to follow suit.

Session 7

Get Inspiration

Read **Romans 12:14-21**. Write down **Romans 12:14** here.

_____
_____
_____

This verse and the subsequent ones (verses 15-21) have been a challenge for me, I must admit. I am learning (trial by fire sometimes) to do all I can to "live at peace with everyone" (v 18).

We cannot go through this broken life without others hurting us, including (and most often) the ones who we love and interact with on a regular basis. Sometimes people simply just rub us the wrong way. We cannot control the actions of others, but we can certainly learn to control our response to them.

One way that is helping me control my response to people is found in **Matthew 5:44**. Record it here:

_____
_____
_____

(I encourage you to read on…powerful and convicting.)

PRAY.

There you have it. That is truly the answer, ladies.

Again, we cannot be "Get Along Girls" in our own human strength. Loving others who are not lovable is hard. We need God to swoop in with His divine intervention. I love what my friend, and fellow writer

Pam Farrel says that she does in tough moments. She says she "*pushes pause and shoots up a prayer*".

We must shoot up a prayer and ask God to help us see other women through the lens that He sees them - as His beautiful, broken daughters, who He is mending and molding into his image.

> We must shoot up a prayer and ask God to help us see other women through the lens that He sees them.

As we learn to listen to his voice and lean into him, we are able to gain the strength we need to love as he loves. If she is his daughter too, then you are her sister! Perhaps blessing this one who persecutes you is just what she needs to be mended.

Often we can so easily skirt through life avoiding the people who have hurt us, threatened us, or put a bad taste in our mouth. There's something to be said for boundaries. It's not wise to make a habit of being around people who constantly cause you to stumble, or "*trip your switch*", as Beth Moore says.

But, the Bible doesn't say ignore the people who persecute you. Not once did Jesus ever say "avoid making eye contact with her at all costs". He doesn't want us to avoid the women we have a difficult time with. No - He says "go and do good" to those who persecute you.

Read **1 Peter 3:8-16**. Record all the ways Peter encourages us to respond to evil or persecution against us.

_____

_____

_____

_____

_____

_____

Now, flip back to **Matthew 5:44** again. This bears repeating. How are we to respond to our enemies?

_____

_____

_____

Remember the phrase "Right feelings follow right actions"?

I firmly believe that when we choose to trust God and obey His Words, although initially forced, the feelings will eventually trail behind. When we retaliate with kindness - doing good to, blessing and praying for the ones we'd rather retaliate with punishment, we will reap rewards that will usher in feelings of peace, joy and love.

Get Intentional

In *Why Can't We All Just Get Along?!* (page #139) I recount a story that Chip Ingram tells about a season in his life that he was challenged to serve a man who was persecuting him. We don't all have a story as dramatic as Chip's. But, we all have people in our lives who have wronged us, or maybe "push our buttons", even unintentionally. Who is your "enemy"? Who do you have unfinished business with? Who irks, irritates, or rubs you the wrong way? Who challenges your patience? Who has offended you? Don't feel that you have to write her name down, but picture her in your mind.

List some things that you can do for this woman. How can you bless the woman you envy, struggle to think well about or makes you feel inferior? She is your tenderness target.

_____
_____
_____
_____

Go and do something good for her. Bless her socks off. Get practical. Engage in a conversation with her. Offer to watch her kids if she's in a bind. Deliver a hot dinner. Compliment with sincerity what she is wearing that day. If that seems daunting, start by writing out a prayer that the Lord would bless her.

_____
_____
_____
_____
_____
_____

If you're feeling brave, follow it up by asking God to make you the answer to that prayer.

There was a time that I could not genuinely pray that God would bless certain women in my life and actually mean it. But, after being obedient and doing what I know the Lord commands me to do, eventually my prayers become heartfelt. The Lord softened my heart as I remained obedient. It can be done, and the Lord will help you.

Remember, He Himself was a "friend of sinners". He loves the exact ones (us all) who directly reject, ignore, spew insults at, take for granted, or could care less about Him.

As you are faithful and obedient, the Lord will bless and refresh you, as you bless and refresh others.

> *"The seeds of good deeds become a tree of life;*
> *a wise person wins friends."*
> **Proverbs 11:30**

Session 8

Ingredient # 7 - A Gram of Gratitude

Get Into It

I remember walking through the cluttered rooms of an estate sale. This was a "score". The owner of the home clearly enjoyed collections and possessions. I had never seen so many linens, trinkets, jewelry, cookbooks or craft supplies. I landed some great buys, which excited me, but I left feeling almost...sad.

The owner clearly found pleasure in things. And yet, there they all were, collecting dust...but she was not there anymore. It was a blatant picture of what we are told - that we all journey from dust to dust and none of our posessions make the journey beyond with us.

> Everything you've been given is not your own.

I will admit that I have not always been a grateful woman. Starting out in adult married life I can remember feeling resentful that I didn't have closet organizers, high end high heels and room in the budget for weekly trips to the salon like many other women did who surrounded me. One of the wealthiest towns in America, Greenwich Connecticut will easily do this to a woman if she's not careful.

It wasn't until I lost nearly every earthly belonging during a move a few years into marriage that I began the daunting journey towards gratitude.

Dan and I lived two and a half years without a home of our own, and that is when God began to do the deep work in me that was necessary in order to understand that everything I have been given is not my own. I've heard it said that scarcity creates gratitude. I would add that it does, only if you allow your heart to remain soft, otherwise it will implant bitterness. It is your choice.

Get Insight

Everything you've been given is not your own. And, the blessings that other women enjoy around you are not their own either. It can all be whisked away in an instant (I discovered this harsh reality), and one day we will leave this earth the way we entered it.

It is easy to get caught up in life's lovely things. Power, popularity and possessions are all quite attractive. But, they also set us up for discontent. We will exist with a "woe is me" mentality when we zoom in on the ones around us who we think have it better in some way.

> We must turn our attention away from others and focus it on Him.

Maybe it's not things that trip you up. Maybe it's the people in your life - their talent, or outward appearance. As we've discussed, when we compare our circumstances to the women around us, we'll consistently either crash land in the middle of a pity party or find ourselves in a mud bath of pride. Both attitudes not only dirty our hearts, but they create division among us. And so, we must turn our attention away from others and focus it on Him.

My husband Dan wrote a song called *Captured Again* years ago, about just this thing. The opening verse says this:

*My mind keeps wandering Lord, to other things I adore
Come again and Capture me.
My life's pursuits can all be so often centered on me
Let my first love burn*

Our "first love" is and should remain, simply, Him. He is enough - no matter what the circumstances. He outshines any spotlight, outweighs any burden, and outlasts every stressful season. A life focused on Him is secure, satisfied and solvent. (Read **Psalms 1:1-3** for a picture of what happens in the life of someone who makes Him their delight and focus)

What makes your mind wander into "Woe is me" territory?

_____
_____
_____
_____

What of your life's pursuits have wedged themselves in between you and God?

_____
_____
_____

Our life's longings can only be quenched by God. Pursuing and paying attention to anything else will always leave a sense of discontentment. But, when we turn our attention to Him, it leaves less time to focus on others. He will never leave us wanting more.

Get Inspiration

Read through **1 Timothy 6:6-10**. What two things does verse 6 tell us will give us great gain?

_____
_____
_____

Godliness and contentment are not the vehicles the world uses to achieve more. But, God promises us that as we strive to be more like Him, and are content with what He provides for us, we will have great gain. The best way to achieve contentment is to understand and practice gratitude until it becomes part of the fabric of our lives.

Turn in your Bible to **James 1:17**. Who gives you every good and perfect gift?

_____
_____
_____

Skip back to **1 Chronicles 16:34**. Why should we give Him thanks?

_____
_____
_____

Now, check out **1 Thessalonians 5:18**. When should we offer up our gratitude?

_____
_____
_____
_____

How does **Philippians 4:6** say we should present any requests we have to God?

_____
_____
_____
_____

What does the following verse promise us as a result?

_____
_____
_____
_____

What is the first thing Paul says in **1 Thessalonians 1:2** as he addresses the Thessalonian church? He sets a great example of how we should be thankful for our sisters in Christ. Record the verse here:

_____
_____
_____
_____

Psalm 9:1 says, *"I will give thanks to the Lord with my whole heart. I will tell of your wonderful deeds."*

In the next section, I want you to do what the Psalmist has done. I want you to tell of all the wonderful things God has done in your life, with a heart of gratitude.

Get Intentional

What are some practical ways you can express your gratitude to God? This is for you to decide. It could be anything from keeping a gratitude journal to giving back by helping others who are less fortunate to expressing your appreciation to the ones you are thankful for.

_____
_____
_____
_____

Follow Paul's lead, and record your gratitude for others here. Who in your life are you thankful for? Who has encouraged you, provided for you, challenged you and helped you grow?

_____
_____
_____
_____

Now, who in your life may not seem like someone you could be thankful for, but perhaps you could view differently as someone who is helping shape you into being more Christlike?

_____
_____
_____
_____

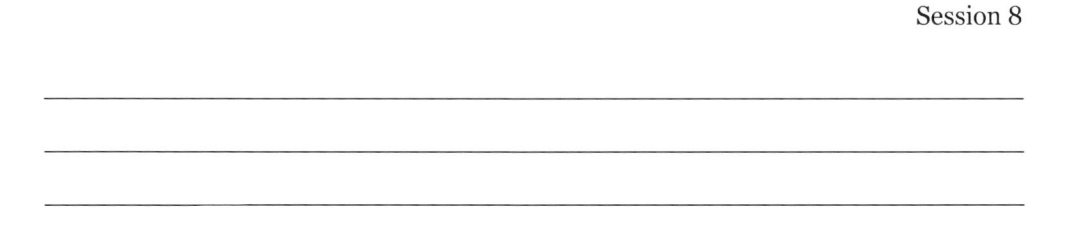

William Arthur Ward says, *"Feeling gratitude and not expressing it is like wrapping a present and not giving it."*. I would add that even if you're not feeling it, give the gift of gratitude anyway, and it will return back to you as an even greater gift.

> *"Turn your eyes upon Jesus, look full in His wonderful face. And the things of earth will grow strangely dim, in the light of His glory and grace."* [8]
> ~ Helen Howarth Lemmel

Ingredient # 8 - A Quart of Confidence

> *Be yourself; everyone else is already taken.*
> ~ Oscar Wilde

Get Into It

I don't need to present you with any statistics or hard facts to prove to you that women struggle with confidence. If we were all in a room together, we'd all have hands raised to the question "Who has ever lacked confidence?".

Building and maintaining confidence feels like a losing battle sometimes. From a critical parent or playground bully, to airbrushed celebrities and social media stars, it certainly is at least an uphill battle to remain confident. But healthy confidence is achievable.

How do you suppose we get there? God's word, of course! He always tells us the truth, and so we can count on what He says about us to be more accurate than what others say, or what we think about ourselves.

Get Insight

Our minds remember negative thoughts much more than positive ones. The average person can feel and recount the bad things that are said and done to them much stronger and more in detail than the many wonderful moments. The Gottman Institute tells us it takes as many as five compliments to counter one criticism, so no wonder we believe and dwell on the worst about ourselves so easily.

> It takes as many as five compliments to counter one criticism.

I imagine if I asked you to write down 5 things you hated about yourself, you'd respond with ease. But, if I challenged you to jot down even 3 things you are proud of and enjoy about yourself, you may struggle.

Where we may feel pathetic, insecure, defeated and loathsome, God looks at us with pride and delight, knowing that He has created us precisely and on purpose - to glorify Him.

Like the manufacturer of a watch knows exactly how and why it ticks, as your maker, God knows you intricately - exactly how you tick. He's the only one who holds the right to define you. So, what does God have to say about you?

Get Inspiration

Let's start with **Psalm 139: 13-18**. Read through, and then write down all it tells you about how you were made and what God thinks about you.

_____
_____
_____
_____

Now, what does **Ephesians 1:4** say about you?

_____
_____
_____
_____

How about **Romans 8:37**?

_____
_____
_____
_____

What does **Philippians 4:19** tell you that God will provide for you?

_____
_____
_____

And so, what can you do, partnered up with God, according to **Phillipians 4:13**?

_____
_____

Write down 2 or 3 statements you have a hard time believing about yourself or God?

_____
_____
_____
_____

I want to remind you that our feelings are flighty and fickle. And, there's a lot of "fake news" circulating out there. Don't always believe those feelings, and certainly don't blindly believe what others tell you above what God says. When faced with harsh and hard words, check them first against God's truth.

If you are feeling unwanted, ugly, inadequate, insecure or like a failure, circle back to these verses. Truly, they only scratch the surface of the confidence available to you through God's word.

He loves you to the cross and back, and He says you are chosen, beautiful, holy, and healed. With His help you can become competent, powerful, wise and free.

> He loves you to the cross and back, and He says you are chosen, beautiful, holy, and healed.

Session 8

Get Intentional

Circle any areas do you lack confidence here below.

- My outer appearance
- My family upbringing
- My intelligence
- My past
- My home
- My talents/abilities
- My mothering

- My relationships
- My sin
- My marriage
- My home
- My singleness
- My financial standing
- Other _____

What lies have you believed about yourself? (Circle them)

- I don't have what it takes/I'll never amount to much
- I'll never be as good as her/why bother trying
- I'll never learn/be better/there's no hope for me
- I'm not who you think I am - I'm a fraud
- I've messed up way too much/I deserve this
- I'm not valuable/worth loving
- I don't deserve blessing in my life
- I can't help the way I am
- I had a shot but I blew it and now this is all there is
- I'm disqualified because of _____
- If I feel something, it must be true

Now, go back in this study, or dig right into your Bible and find God's truth that combats at least two or three of the lies you have believed about yourself. Write the truth down here.

_____
_____
_____
_____
_____
_____
_____
_____
_____
_____

Who do you lack confidence around, and how can God's Word equip you to remain confident, even in their presence?

> Tuck God's word into your heart and mind, so that you can find it easily when you need it most.

I believe the best way is to tuck God's word into your heart and mind, so that you can find it easily when you need it most. One way I do that is to keep note cards with scripture written on it handy in my purse, on my kitchen counter and even in my car - wherever it is in front of me. I've even been known to walk out of Hobby Lobby with some wall art or a notepad that will remind me of what God says.

The best way to do that though, is to memorize it! I challenge you to memorize two verses this week that will build your confidence both in

God and in yourself. What will those verses be?

1. _____
   _____
   _____
   _____
   _____

2. _____
   _____
   _____
   _____
   _____

As we become confident women, understanding who God has created us to be and believing that we are as valuable as we really are, we develop the ability to build up the women around us. We are able to cheer others on in their God-given gifts. This is crucial because it promotes unity. And, we can do much much more together than we ever could apart.

I love the words of Vista M. Kelly: *"Snowflakes are one of nature's most fragile things, but just look at what they can do when they stick together."*[9] When you feel fragile, run to God, and then run to each other - and as you do, you will become an avalanche of love.

> *"Self confidence has limited potential. God confidence has unlimited possibility"* ~ Renee Swope

Session 9

Consequences of Disunity

I firmly believe that God's word has given you the tools to be genuinely woven together with your sisters in Christ. I pray that this study has offered a glimmer of hope that you really all can get along in every way. If you've yet to be challenged to do so, I know this final section of the study will ignite a fire in you to take God at His Word. I would be remiss if I did not disclose the results and realities of not "getting along."

How will our lives be affected when we choose not to live in harmony with one another? What are the ramifications of allowing ourselves to remain bound in our personal issues, which hinder healthy relationships? Here are a few of the major consequences that surely await us when we choose not to get along...

1 - Isolation

Get Into It

I follow the incredible Lysa Terkeurst on Instagram. The other day she posted these words:

> *"If the enemy can isolate us, He can influence us."*

Man, has he tried these tactics on me before. And, when he's succeeded, he's had a heyday on my thought life. Solitary confinement truly is a form of punishment. It is in the quietness of our own thoughts that the devil can convince us of everything evil.

> Isolation is exactly where our enemy wants us.

This is exactly where the enemy wants to keep us... alone.

The spoilers we tackle in this Bible Study all stem from over focusing on, and even an obsession with self. A life that focuses on self is a surefire way of keeping distance from others. Our insecurities put up walls and shut us out from genuine intimacy with each other. Pride hammers up the same barriers. Unforgiveness, competition, envy, jealousy, judging, misunderstanding...they all lead us down the path to isolation.

Get Insight

Whether you're a stay at home mom, the only woman surrounded by men in your corporate community, new to town and haven't found your "people" yet, or stuck caring for an elderly parent around the clock, you know the discouraging place of Isolation. But whatever we are walking through, we need each other desperately.

And yet, often, our pride prevents us from requesting help or simply saying "I need you".

Worse, when we let the relationship spoilers interfere, we are doomed to become vulnerable to the ill effects of isolation. Here are just a few:

- More likely to feel depressed and anxious and develop paranoia
- More likely to develop illness

Session 9

- Less ability to handle stress
- Long term mental health issues

Read this alarming excerpt from the website Science Alert:

> "People placed in isolation may also experience hallucinations. The lack of stimuli causes people to misattribute internal thoughts and feelings as occurring in the outer environment. Essentially, *hallucinations* happen because of a lack of brain stimulation....In fact, Alati revealed he began experiencing hallucinations by his third day in isolation, ranging from seeing the room fill up with bubbles, to imagining that the ceiling had opened up to show him a starry sky.
>
> People in total isolation may also feel that there is a *ghostly presence or someone watching them*..... Natascha Kampusch – an Austrian woman who was kidnapped at the age of ten and held captive in a cellar for eight years – noted in her biography that the lack of light and human contact *mentally* weakened her. She also reported that endless hours and days spent completely isolated made her *susceptible to her captor's orders and manipulations*."[10] (emphasis mine)

Go through and read the italicized portions of this excerpt, and then write those words down below.

_____
_____
_____
_____
_____

Isolation is exactly where our enemy wants us, because he knows it is where he has the best chance to skew our thoughts, make us see what is not there, think what is not true, follow his orders and fall prey to his manipulations. According to these accounts, it seems as though our enemy becomes more loud and clear and present in our isolation.

Get Inspiration

Let's look at the other dark and dangerous places the Bible tells us that isolation leads us:

Read **Proverbs 18:1** My version says, "Whoever isolates himself seeks his own desire; he breaks out against all sound judgement." Jot down your version here:

_____
_____
_____
_____

Some versions say *"unfriendly people"* isolate themselves. Chew on that.

What does part B of the verse say will happen to those people?

_____
_____

When we isolate ourselves, we rob ourselves of the opportunity for people to speak wisdom into our lives. We handicap our growth. We dull the weapons that help us fight off the enemy.

Proverbs 27:17 tells us that "iron sharpens iron, so one person sharpens another." If we do not have any iron to sharpen us, we become ineffective, weak, and definitely dull.

On the other hand, here is just one reason God tells us to make sure we join together:

Copy out **Hebrews 10:24-25** here:

_____

_____

_____

_____

And, listen to the words of Solomon in Ecclesiastes:

> *Two are better than one,*
>   *because they have a good return for their labor:*
> *If either of them falls down,*
>   *one can help the other up.*
> *But pity anyone who falls*
>   *and has no one to help them up.*
> *Also, if two lie down together, they will keep warm.*
>   *But how can one keep warm alone?*
> *Though one may be overpowered,*
>   *two can defend themselves.*
> *A cord of three strands is not quickly broken.*
>   **Ecc. 4:9-12**

God created us to be together - to encourage, edify, challenge (sharpen) and love one another. Being alone gives the devil opportunity to tempt, distract, lie and accomplish his other plans against you. We need to do everything we can to trample down the walls around us and reach out for one another. Let's do that now.

Get Intentional

How have I isolated myself from the women around me? Has it been insecurity, pride, unresolved issues?

_____
_____
_____
_____

Who can I reach out to today to enjoy and benefit from the sense of connection that comes from face to face quality time with others?

_____
_____
_____

Who needs me to reach out to them today, to rescue them from the punishment of loneliness and the evils of isolation?

_____
_____
_____

"The worst cruelty that can be inflicted on a human being is isolation"
~ Sukarno

Session 9

2 - Disobedience

Get Into It

When we allow the spoilers that we have studied here to rule our thoughts and actions, they become sin. We must take ownership that these are not just "hang ups", weakness or the enemy's fault.

Not only will we be isolated from others, but our sin of not "getting along" separates us from God. This is why God hates sin. He wants nothing between us and Him.

> God takes it personally, how we treat one another.

It is frightening to realize, yet we must grasp that "Your iniquities have separated you from your God; your sins have hidden His face from you, so that He will not hear" (**Isaiah 59:2**; see also **Isaiah 13:11**; **Jeremiah 5:25**).

It is crucial to understand that when we allow the spoilers to keep us from walking in obedience, we impede not only our connection with other women, but with God, our life-source. This has monumental implications.

Get Insight

God takes it personally how we treat one another, since we are his daughters. In the same way that children resemble their parents, we resemble Him. So, when He looks at each of us, He sees Himself. I have two kids - sweetest boys on planet earth in all their noisy, stinky, dirty glory. If you mess with them, you mess with me. If you aren't treating them right, I'm going to have something to say (or do) about it.

> Our disobedience doesn't just negatively affect us, it touches everyone around us.

Similarly, if we aren't "getting along" with the women around us God has strong feelings about that. You mess with His little girl, you mess with Him. If you backstab, gossip, speak hurtful damaging words, hold a grudge or even just harbor negative thoughts towards another woman, you've done that against God. Also, if you are destroying yourself in any way, He will do everything He can to swoop in and put a halt to that as well.

Our Heavenly Father has strong feelings about His daughters and has something to say about sin that's directed towards them. We need to stay tuned in to His voice so he can caution us when we're walking down a dangerous path of disobedience.

Get Inspiration

According to **James 1:14-15**, what does disobedience (being led astray by our own desires) lead to?

_____

_____

Name at least one person/people group we have studied that were led away by their own sinful desires, became tangled up in their own sin, and then suffered the consequences. Then, turn to **Genesis 19** to read the result of Lot's wife's disobedience. What were Lot and his wife instructed to do in verse 17? _____

_____

What became of Lot's wife in verse 26? Why?

_____

_____

_____

_____

Beginning in the Garden of Eden with Eve, there are many Biblical examples of women who faced the consequences of disobedience. Let their example serve as a stark reminder that when we choose to walk in disobedience, there will be a painful price to pay.

Look up the instructions the Apostle Paul gave to two women (Euodia and Syntyche) in the church of Philipi who were clearly in a dispute and not getting along. You can find his words here:

Philippians 4:2-3

_____

_____

_____

_____

Notice at the end of verse three, that these women had labored to advance the gospel, and who's names, Paul believed, were written in the book of life. Yet, Paul still felt it important to address their discord and disobedience in the opening sentences of his letter, because he knew that internal disunity will seriously undermine the church.

Our disobedience doesn't just negatively affect us, it touches everyone around us.

On the flip side, what does **Deuteronomy 5:33** say will happen when we walk in the ways God has commanded us?

_____

_____

_____

Be comforted, knowing this: **Proverbs 3:12** says *"The Lord Disciplines those He loves"*. When God disciplines us for our disobedience, He has a firm hand of love. Even more so than we are concerned for our own children's wellbeing, our Heavenly Father wants His very best for us. Discipline is His method used to course correct.

Wonderfully, He tells us that His mercies are new every morning. We get a fresh start every day to make things right between ourselves and God - and with each other. (**Lamentations 3:22-23**)

Get Intentional

I cannot promise you that your disobedience won't have consequences. Let me give you an opportunity though, to make things right and take the first step to walking in obedience to Christ when it comes to your relationships.

Write down the "spoilers" that have caused you to walk in disobedience. Perhaps there are specific events or people that come to mind, or maybe they are just a constant struggle for you.

_____

_____

_____

_____

Now that you've identified those things, pray a prayer of repentance (a decision to turn away from those things), and ask The Lord to reconcile yourself to others and to Him. He is waiting to hear from you...

_____
_____
_____
_____

Thank you God, that no matter our disobedience, when we are remorseful and repentant, you graciously and willingly forgive and restore our relationship with you and help us to restore our relationships with one another. Amen.

> *"Whoever heeds discipline shows the way to life, but whoever ignores correction leads others astray."*
> **Proverbs 10:17**

3 Missing Out on God's Blessing

Get Into It

Throughout *Why Can't We All Just Get Along?!*, I share the incredible story of God turning my heart from cold and callous towards a woman, to one that is warm and loving. The relationship I have with that woman today is one filled to the brim and overflowing with abundant blessing. She is single handedly the most influential woman in my life spiritually and has mentored me into who I am today. I don't want to think about all that I'd missed out on if I had kept my heart at a distance from hers.

> God is good on His word when it comes to blessing people who do things His way.

God is exceedingly gracious beyond our understanding. When we get things wrong, He always offers a way to make it right. The truth is though, that God is also good on His word when it comes to blessing people who do things His way. We find in God's word, a recurring pattern of cause and effect, or what it refers to as "sowing and reaping".

Countless times in scripture we see God use "cause and effect" statements like "If you do this, then you will receive that". Here are a couple examples:

"If you are willing and obedient, you shall eat the good of the land; but if you refuse and rebel, you shall be eaten by the sword." **Isaiah 1:19, 20**

"Those who plow iniquity and sow trouble reap the same." **Job 4:8**

Look up the following verses, and then record the "cause and effect", or the "sowing and reaping" statement:

John 14:23 _____
_____
_____

Session 9

2 Corinthians 9:6 _____

_____

_____

Proverbs 3:5-6 _____

_____

_____

Proverbs 22:8a _____

_____

_____

2 Chronicles 26:5 _____

_____

_____

Psalm 126:5-6 _____

_____

_____

Clearly, there are always consequences or blessings, depending on our actions, and the motivations that drive them. For further convincing, I encourage you to check out **Deuteronomy 28**! If we allow the "spoilers" to rule our thoughts, attitudes, behaviors, and interactions with the people around us, it will barricade the tidal wave of blessing that God is wanting to heavily shower upon us.

As we wrap up this study, I encourage you to take stock of your life and relationships, and imagine the blessing that would come your way if, in that relationship, you lived in accordance with God's word, and how He's directing you to live. The final section of this study will shed light on the importance of unity, and the reasons why God wants us to "get along".

> *"For you bless the righteous, O Lord; you cover him with favor as a shield".* **Psalm 5:12**

Session 10

Unity

Get Into It

This is it, ladies. The crux of the matter. Unity is where we're landing this plane, and I hope it is our final destination. I pray that unity is the major overarching fruit grown out of this Bible Study.

The Church is sometimes referred to as "The Bride of Christ." (**2 Corinthians 11:2**, **Revelation 19:7-9 and 21:9**). Everyone is drawn to a beautiful bride. All eyes are on her as she walks down the aisle. Can you imagine the horror, however, of seeing a beat up, black eye'd, swollen lipped, torn dressed bride coming towards her groom? The sight would make you want to look away, and yet, you wouldn't be able to.

> Our unity will convince unbelievers that they need Jesus.

This is what the world sees when we are not unified - a bruised up, bloodied bride. What's worse is, all to often, these wounds are self inflicted from "friendly fire". But, when we love like Christ - the kind of love that the world can't acheive on it's own, the onlookers will be drawn in and join us down the aisle.

Get Insight

More than our pastor's powerful preaching, our churches progressive programs or our clever points and arguments, our *unity* will convince unbelievers that they need Jesus. Frankly, they won't ever want Him if what they see is a bunch of disgruntled and disunified Christ followers not getting along.

I want to remind you of the words found in **John 13:34-35**. After washing the disciples feet, and before He would be taken away to be tortured for them, Jesus shared His overarching priority for those He trusted to represent him.

> *"A new commandment I give to you, that you love one another: just as I have loved you, you are also to love one another. By this all people will know that you are my disciples; if you have love for one another."*

I see all too often, public forum Facebook posts filled with Christ's disciples busy debating, disputing, condemning and crucifying. This is indicative of what is taking place within church walls. And, all I can think about are those gazelle's locking horns while their real enemy - that Lion - is coming in for attack, all while the onlookers are taking it all in.

Get Inspiration

God takes our solidarity seriously. Throughout scripture, He or His apostles practically please with Christ followers to live at peace and in harmony, without divisions. Write down the following exhortations:

Ephesians 4:1-3 _____

_____

_____

Philippians 2:2 _____
_____
_____

1 Peter 3:8 _____
_____
_____

1 Corinthians 1:10 _____
_____
_____

2 Corinthians 13:11 _____
_____
_____

As you can see, it is reiterated over and over that the church must be unified. But, why!? Does it really matter if there are quarrels among us? I mean, we're human right!? Aren't we going to disagree from time to time? If we dance with anyone long enough, we're bound to step on their toes.

> Our lives are on display

Yes, it's true that there will always be issues to deal with, heads will butt and personalities will clash - but it is how we handle these moments and how we treat one another through the process that matters. Our lives are on display, ladies. And, if we can't figure out how to get along, the watching world will not be convinced of God's power.

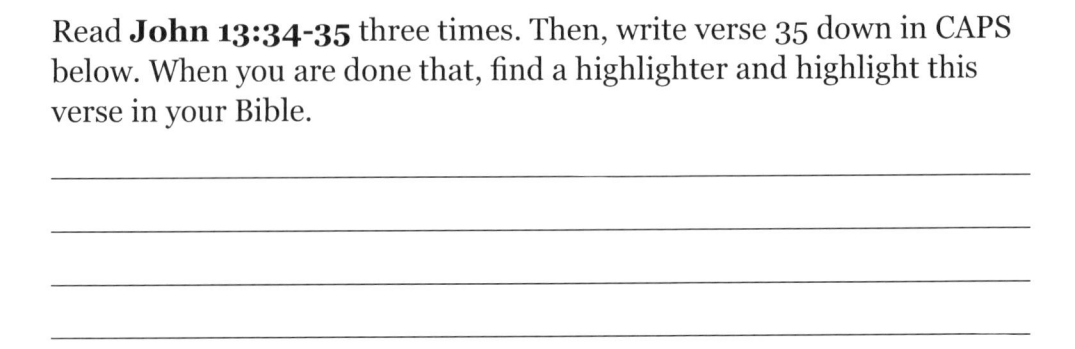

Read **John 13:34-35** three times. Then, write verse 35 down in CAPS below. When you are done that, find a highlighter and highlight this verse in your Bible.

_____
_____
_____
_____

There you have it. This is why we must all get along!

Here are a few more reasons why it is good that we come together in heart and mind:

- We don't function as well separately as we do together
    (**Romans 12:4-5**)
- There is power in the prayers of those who join together
    (**Matthew 18:20**)
- We make each other better by sharpening each other
    (**Proverbs 27:17**)
- We can mentor and teach one another by our examples
    (**Titus 2:3-5**)

Together, we are stronger. It's that simple.

Session 10

Get Intentional

What women in your life have been a good example to you? Who have you learned and grown from, simply by watching them in action? Jot their names down here, with a heart beside them:

_____
_____

Who have you joined in prayer with, or teamed up with to accomplish something great and bigger than yourselves??

_____
_____

Who challenges, guides and encourages you in your faith journey?

_____
_____

Now, who can you challenge, encourage and help guide? Who can you pray with and pray for? Who can you be a positive example to? Write her name here:

_____
_____

Now, write a prayer of gratitude for the women that God has placed in your life along the way, and ask God to show you how you can be a blessing to others.

_____
_____
_____
_____

_____
_____
_____
_____
_____
_____
_____
_____

If you've struggled to fill in these lines, it's time to fight for your relationships - not against each other. It is time to prioritize the person over her problem. It's time to fight for unity - not the "win".

God, how good and pleasant it is when women dwell in unity (**Psalm 133:1**). You are pleased and glorified when we all "get along". Help us to become more like you, as we learn to become unified with one another. In Jesus name, Amen.

> *"May our dependably steady and warmly personal God develop maturity in you so that you get along with each other as well as Jesus gets along with us all. Then we will be a choir - not our voices only, but our very lives singing in harmony in a stunning anthem to the God and Father of our Master Jesus!"*
> **Romans 15:1-7** *(The Message)*

ENDNOTES

1. Carey Neiwhof, Didn't See It Coming, (Crown Publishing Group 2018) p. 116
2. https://citatis.com/a1585/11cbdd/
3. C.S. Lewis, Mere Christianity, (Geoffrey Bles (UK) Macmillian Publishers Harper Collins 1952) p. 124
4. Carey Nieuwof, Didn't See It Coming, (Crown Publishing Group 2018) p. 121
5. Lysa Terkeurst, Uninvited, (Thomas Nelson Books Harper Collins 2016) p.27-28
6. Donald Miller, Scary Close (Thomas Nelson 2015) p. 65
7. Martin Luther King Jr., Strength to Love (Fortress Press 2010) p. 26-27
8. Helen Howarth Lemmel, Turn Your Eyes Upon Jesus, Glad Songs 1922
9. Vista M. Kelly, https://www.quotery.com/authors/vista-m-kelly
10. Science Alert Website https://www.sciencealert.com/isolation-has-profound-effects-on-the-human-body-and-brain-here-s-what-happens

THE GET ALONG TRIO

The book that started it all. Begin your journey here or catch up now!

GETALONGGIRL.COM

Go even deeper into The Word, make it personal, and grow!

Grab The Get Along Video Group Guide! Short videos from Danielle designed to turn the guide you're holding into the perfect small-group study! Get it at:

GETALONGGUIDE.COM

ABOUT THE AUTHOR

Danielle Macaulay is an author, blogger, speaker and television personality on the marriage television show, *A Better Us*.

She is passionate about her marriage to her husband, recording artist Dan Macaulay, her two young boys, Keaton and Braden, and about helping women grow in their faith (she isn't afraid to admit she is also passionate about donuts, Hallmark movies and the spa).

She provides regular nourishment for both your body and soul at her popular blog spot **frommilktomeat.com** and offers families spiritual nourishment and kid friendly recipes in her children's meal time devotional, *Table Talk: Family Dinner Devos*.

To book Danielle to speak at your event, contact:
info@daniellemacaulay.com

/FromMilkToMeat

/DanielleMacaulay80

OTHER WEBSITES TO CHECK OUT

- frommilktomeat.com
- getalonguide.com
- getalonggirl.com
- danmac.org
- abetterus.tv

ALSO FROM DANIELLE:

TABLETALKDEVOS.COM
Get your family talking about things that matter!

Manufactured by Amazon.ca
Bolton, ON

14715434R00090